SURRENDERING TO

MOTHERHOOD

SURRENDERING TO
MOTHERHOOD

Losing Your Mind,
Finding Your Soul

IRIS KRASNOW

HYPERION

NEW YORK

Library of Congress Cataloging-in-Publication Data
Krasnow, Iris.
Surrendering to motherhood : losing your mind, finding your soul /
Iris Krasnow.
p. cm.
ISBN 0–7868–6217–3
1. Krasnow, Iris. 2. Mothers—United States—Biography.
3. Motherhood. 4. Motherhood—Psychological aspects. I. Title.
HQ759.K725 1997
649'.1—dc20   96–30764
                                                                    CIP

Paperback ISBN: 0-7868-8318-9

Designed by Jill Gogal

FIRST PAPERBACK EDITION

10 9 8 7 6 5 4 3

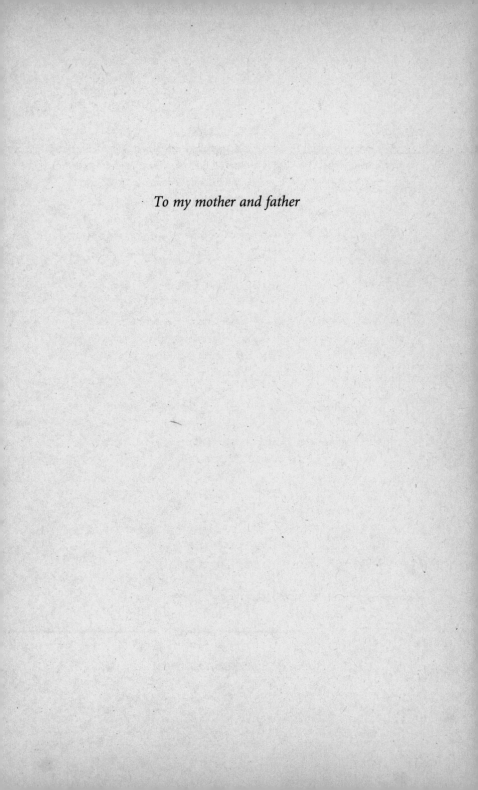

To my mother and father

Acknowledgments

There are many, many people who helped shape this work. I'd like to first thank my editor at the *Washington Post*, Peggy Hackman, who gave me the freedom back in the fall of 1994 to write a story for her Style Plus section called "Surrendering to Motherhood." After reading this raw and heartfelt article, Miramax chief Bob Weinstein encouraged me to unleash and enlarge the power of four small sons into book form. I will forever be grateful for the opportunity to spend nearly two years writing about my passion.

My coach and comrade during the process was my editor Susan Dalsimer, the wise, funny, exacting, and patient vice-president of Miramax Books. This mother of fourteen-year-old Sophie and eleven-year-old Sam has my unwavering admiration and appreciation. I'd also like to thank my longtime Chicago friend John Rasmus, now the editor of *Men's Journal*, who agreed to provide us with a male view of the book. John offered criticism that led to some of the most important changes made. Peggy Cooper Cafritz and Siobhan Hannas were good enough to offer further insights and advice. And my sister, Fran, was wonderful as I neared the finish line, helping me to sharpen and clarify.

Surrendering to Motherhood is about achieving wholeness through the tight web of family, something I learned from my own mother and father, who constantly reminded me that my brother, Greg, and sister would be the best friends I ever had. My parents turned out to be right. That gift of unconditional love gave me the hunger and faith to bring my own children into the world. To the Krasnow family from which I sprang and to the Krasnow-Anthony family which I helped create, you are the heart of *Surrendering to Motherhood*. My steadfast architect husband, Chuck, gets the credit for setting the foundation for my dreams.

You cannot surrender to motherhood without great girl-friends with whom you can vent. I am grateful to be surrounded by a far-flung and devoted circle of females who never fail to listen and to laugh. Thank you for humoring me through all of life's passages. Some of these links go back twenty and thirty years, with Terri Rubin, Simone Gould, Debbie Wolman, Josette Shiner, Ellyn Arnstein, Amy Rudnick, Margery Eagan, Sarah Haskell, and Janet Sullivan.

My enduring gratitude also goes to Bernice, Mary, Marie, Cathy, Liz, and Berna. Over the years these gentle and loyal women have cared for our sons as if they were their own. They have made it possible for a mother to write at home while her children are playing in the next room. And to my agent Jan Miller, a friend of sixteen years, you are an astonishing person who knows how to make things happen.

Iris Krasnow

Life is a struggle for joy all along the way. May I fight to win the battle on the very spot where I am now.
—Paramahansa Yogananda

Surrendering to Motherhood

Prologue:
Surrendering to Motherhood

I am the mother of four little boys. "No girls, just five boys and a mommy," as four-year-old Isaac likes to say. As I complete the final pages of this book about women I am imagining what I would like to tell a twenty-year-old daughter, if I had one, of my lifelong search to find peace and God and happiness.

I would take her on my whole convoluted journey, through Buddhism and meditation and macrobiotics and est and body building and journalism. I'd tell her what it was like to come of age at the onset of feminism and the sexual revolution, of the euphoria and agony that resulted from being freed to sort through a staggering array of choices in life and love. I'd talk to her about the generational angst that sprung from attempting to Have It All.

I would reveal that when I was her age I wanted to be stronger and smarter than my housewife mother, that my outrage at the oppression of women stuck in their kitchens helped turn me into a savvy Woman of the World who was determined never to become stagnant and subservient.

I would pull from the shelf my yellowed *Be Here Now*, Baba Ram Dass's 1971 book on finding enlightenment by plunging yourself into the present that I read as a college student until the pages fell out. I'd admit to her that *Be Here Now* didn't work; that I grew into a woman ablaze with ambition who was always racing past the Now to try and get somewhere better, a woman who was after the perfect job, the perfect body, and the perfect relationship all at once.

Then I would tell my daughter that no matter how high I climbed, what I craved in the deepest cave of my heart was a good man to marry and to have a bunch of kids.

I would stop and smile and sigh and probably start crying as I shared the extraordinary details of the day I had my first child, and of the chaos that came after when three more babies were born shortly thereafter. I would tell her how this puppy pack of boys would derail my career but link me inexorably to my soul and to the Almighty and to the present and to the forever. I would describe how these wriggly children captured me in the fleeting moment that is now, and ultimately drew me toward the peace I had always tried desperately to reach.

I would share that my dream for her as a woman was to live a substantial life, a life in which she was productive and passionate and charitable and open-minded. I would pass on what my parents told me: You can be whatever you want to be if you work hard and never give up. But I'd attach this personal addendum: Don't let your profession be an obstacle to knowing and loving your family; raising good kids is a noble goal in itself.

I would then draw her close and tell her that I may be able to save her a few lost years if she heeded these words: When the ancient and instinctive desire to become a mother starts surging, follow your gut, go for that lasting high, even if it means taking some of the steam out of a Hot Career and giving up adrenaline-laced adventures.

I would tell her that should she decide to make children her priority she should never feel as if she was failing the feminist cause. Because her liberated mother had been independent and successful and had delayed marriage until the age of thirty-three, and here is what she had found: that after years of trying to find power in various gurus and exotic boyfriends, in interviews with movie stars, senators, and even a queen, surrendering to motherhood was the most liberating and powerful thing she had ever done in her life.

I would reminisce about sitting in San Francisco cafes in Indian-print skirts and halter tops with my college pals and talking about going everywhere and being everything and trying everything and being the best of all. Then I'd shrug and laugh and admit that two decades later I was content to just sit at my kitchen table, and that what I wanted most of all was to be a great mom. I'd warn her that being a mother would suck her dry, and that she may fight it and resent it and run away from it like me. But that eventually she would come back, that she should come back, fully and forcefully, and she, too, would discover a primal and breathtaking happiness.

Alas, there is no daughter in my nest, but the experiences I allude to that rocked some sense into me over the years certainly are not gender-specific. My boys will hear plenty about loving too much and living too outrageously and right turns and wrong turns made along the way. And, hopefully, in these tales of old, they will learn something about What Really Matters in the long haul. My women friends always remind me that my primary job as the mother of four sons is to turn out sensitive and nurturing males, and I take this assignment quite seriously. I work very hard, every day, toward building good boys and great men, men who will be tender and flexible and responsible husbands, men who will become fathers who will love their children with all their might.

I cannot wait until the day comes that I can hand my sons this book about brothers Theo, Isaac, Jack, and Zane, that tracks how they pushed their Type A mother into this sweet, sweet place. They will read my message over and over: If you choose to become a parent, Be There. Childhood is over in an eye blink; you don't want to miss the chance to love fully and to feel whole and to be fully loved, sensations no job can ever give you.

I do not claim to be a perfect model of motherhood; I

am a mother who tries every day to be better than the day before. Note the "Surrendering" in the title rather than "Surrendered"; adapting to motherhood is still a process, it is not a completed act.

I have not surrendered. I am surrendering. I still fumble and I get frustrated; there are moments when I miss the intoxication of The Chase. I hear of feature-writing slots open at Washington bureaus of national magazines that entice me, of press secretary positions with exciting members of Congress. I go through intense longings to apply for these jobs, our family could use the extra money, my brain could use the stimulation, my ego could use the strokes. I would love to get out of the house a few hours of the day in my black Gap suit.

Two children ago, I might have been able to, but not with four under the age of six in my charge. I'm sure many of you have been in this same predicament: some alluring professional opportunity is dangled in front of you, perhaps on a day when your kids have been a pain, and you want nothing more than to go back to your glamorous career. But then you snap back into the glorious present where a son is bringing you *The Little Engine That Could* to read aloud and his baby brother is asleep in your lap and you know that Right Here Right Now you need to be at home as much as they need you to be there, perhaps even more.

One woman I know complains that her two toddler girls call their baby-sitter "Mama," and it's very upsetting to her. My friend is a woman whose husband makes a good living, and whose family would still thrive if she cut back on her hours, which she would be able to do as a computer consultant. She told me that money has nothing to do with her desire to be Out There in the World. As she puts it: "My sense of self needs more than 'Mother' as a job title."

Well, I'm no stranger to that type of thinking—a lot of women who wanted everything and got most of it know what she's talking about. For me, the importance of downsizing Self and yielding more and more to my kids did not come to me in a volcanic burst of altruism and clarity. I began to give in because, with four small children, I literally couldn't do anything else but respond to their needs. Because of the swoop of fertile fate that was ours I was forced to stop, and with that came surrender, and with that came an ability to Be Where I Was When I Was There.

During the blizzard of 1996 my good friend Olvia Demetriou, an architect and interior designer and mother of two young sons, called and told me how thrilled she was that she couldn't leave her house. "Isn't it great to have just stopped?" Olvia remarked. "To stop the madness, to stop the running around, to be able to play in the snow with the kids and not worry that you have to be somewhere else." Olvia had two restaurant projects going at the time, and she'd been working killer hours to make her deadlines. I told her that I had stopped a couple of years ago, but I often envied the madness she experienced being caught up in her profession.

"You're lucky to be where you are," she told me. "We all want what we don't have."

I told her that I wanted what I had, *and* I also wanted a piece of what she had.

She laughed and told me that this one would really get me: At a dinner party that past Saturday night she was seated next to George Stephanopoulos, and that he was very witty and very handsome and very interesting. I hung up the phone and looked at the dinner party attended by four filthy boys in my own kitchen. The menu was by Stouffer's, spinach soufflé, and there was green, green, everywhere, in all of our hair, on the floor, even a glob on the window. What would George Stephanopoulos think of this scene?

There are constant flickers of wanting to be chatting up prominent people like I used to; the election of 1996 was the first since 1984 that I had no part in covering as a journalist. But then I'm slammed back into What Is and out of panging for What Is Not by four kids screeching around the kitchen, and by my morning *Washington Post* where I stumble upon this remarkable quote from George Bush: "I used to be the president of the United States. Now I am a happy dad and granddad—that's it. That's the way it should be."

Once the most powerful person in the country, and one of the most powerful people in the world, George Bush hammered home what I am thankfully discovering more and more to be true: In our families lies our greatest fulfillment and satisfaction.

In the end, I do not have seven habits to pass on that lead to highly successful mothering. Nor can I list ten stupid things parents do to mess up their families. But after writing some two hundred pages on my children and the struggles of my own heart, I do have one: Be There. Then you'll get to hear all the extraordinary things that come out of your children's mouths. For me that means listening to questions like:

"If God makes all the people, then who makes God?"

"Can God put 1997 on rewind? I had a lot of fun this year."

I had a lot of fun, too. And there's lots more to come, of this I am certain. This afternoon we are sitting on a dock lowering wire-mesh pots into the river to catch succulent bluecrabs for dinner, and I'm looking at four children with Fudgsicle on their faces. And I am overcome, as I am dozens of times every day, by a Knowing that there is nowhere I want to be other than where I am.

THE CLIMB

➚➛

For as long as I can remember I have been wrestling to find something that would give meaning to my life, something to feed my spiritual hunger, soothe my churning psyche, to ground me in the Now. At the age of forty-one, I look back through my diaries and see how I have never wavered from this often painful quest, a journey to know myself, to like myself, to be content with what was rather than spinning in angst over what could be. A poem I wrote in 1968, my first year at Oak Park-River Forest High School near Chicago, starts out like this: "I pondered a question for what seemed to be a year. The question is quite simple: What am I doing here? I read and write and talk and walk, but these to no avail. For when I know not why or who it is myself I fail."

I was always the person who, wherever I was, thought I should be somewhere else.

Just out of braces and with long, straight hair achieved by sleeping on curlers of orange juice cans, I should have been content with the fun and fluff that is youth, not penning dark poetry. Yet I felt lost in a freshman class of more than a thousand, too cool for the girls in Villager kilts, not cool enough for the artsy crowd who listened to Jimi Hendrix and smoked Oak Park's first pot. Even with the exhilaration that comes with the many milestones of high school—the first prone make-out session, first Sloe Gin Fizz stupor, first car keys, first love—I was aching to fill an emptiness deep inside. Some distraction came from cheerleading and going steady with the hulky tight end of the varsity football team. This dark, silent, mustached man took me on dates to drive-in movies and shared his bottles of pink Ripple and packs of Kool cigarettes.

While being a cheerleader is a universal girlhood fantasy, flipping around in an orange and navy blue thigh-high skirt, orange hair ribbons flying, usually made me feel silly. During basketball season, our squad would assemble into a pyramid and I would take center stage on the gymnasium floor and slide into the Chinese splits. Frozen smile in place, one arm on my hip, the other held high and rigid, I had one strong and recurring realization: I am not this person. This is my first memory of knowing that what the Buddhists call True Nature was separate from the Self who was acting out her life. What I could never have imagined back then at fifteen was just how long it would take to discover the wholeness and harmony I was looking for. I was to experience a duality of self again and again as I fumbled through high school, college, and beyond, often from being in relationships that were clearly wrong, or hanging around a group for camaraderie only to be hit by a profound loneliness.

Even as a young girl, I always felt different. Most of my friends from nursery school through high school were Catholic, as was nearly half the village of 65,000. The Krasnows were among the 2 percent of the population in the village who were Jewish. Despite these small numbers, I was made acutely aware of my roots by a mother who fled the Nazis and her Warsaw home for Paris. Her immediate family was killed.

The Holocaust permeated our lives, it made my mother cry often, it made her steely when we cried over the minor crises most kids cry over. Had we lived in one of the northern suburbs of Chicago like Lincolnwood, there would have been lots of other Jewish kids with parents who talked funny and dwelled on the Holocaust. But Helene Krasnow seemed to be the only haunted Jew around, and she was ours, and there was no escape.

No one in Oak Park talked like she talked. The only people I knew who had rumbly accents like my mother were people I was related to. On my father's side: Grandma Margaret, Uncle Louie, Aunt Minnie—all from Kiev. And on my mother's side: Uncle Morris, Aunt Lila, and cousin Jacques, from Poland. A survivor of three death camps, Jacques's arm is branded with a blue number. This assemblage of foreigners made me feel proud and strange.

My mother survived by living in the Paris home of a Catholic woman who befriended her. When the Germans were ghettoizing the Jews of Warsaw, my grandmother encouraged her youngest daughter Helene, whose next sibling was sixteen years older, to flee their hometown and the family. My grandmother told her: "I am too old to move. Your sister and brother are settled here with their children. Go, we will find you when this is over." Helene listened to her mother, and at sixteen set out for Paris alone, a city she would live in for the next sixteen years. Her mother, a brother, sister, five nieces, and a nephew she left behind were killed.

My father, Theodore Krasnow, was raised in the Austin neighborhood on the west side of Chicago. His father, Henry Krasnow, born Krasnowsky in Odessa, was one of the first Russian doctors in Chicago, emigrating to America at the turn of the century. My grandmother, from near Kiev, was a nurse at Cook County Hospital. When he was a skinny adolescent of fifteen, my dad started his first company, a photography business called Edgewater Concessions. Stalking the beaches of Lake Michigan with his bulky camera over his shoulder and shooting pictures of sunbathers helped put him through Northwestern University business school. In 1945, he cofounded Marvel Metal Products Company, a housewares firm that started out making metal wastebaskets and tissue boxes in a small garage shop.

When the war ended, my mother applied for a visa to the United States but her immigration papers were stalled for several years. Finally, in 1951, she was able to join her brother Morris, who had moved to Chicago before the war. She got a job selling French perfume at Saks Fifth Avenue on Michigan Avenue, and was introduced to my father on a blind date. He communicated to her in high school French, and she answered in the English she was learning in night classes. They married less than a year later.

Marvel Metal grew into one of the country's leading manufacturers of office and computer furniture. Yet the Depression that sculpted my parents' characters continued to harness their spending habits. Self-conscious about the opulence of some of the new generation of Jews in America, my father was most comfortable in the middle class of Oak Park. When a cousin was visiting our home and parked his Cadillac in the driveway, a teenage boy from across the street asked me who owned the "Jew canoe." That stung, and I became self-conscious, too. My father drove Oldsmobiles until the day he died in 1986.

Other events made me sensitive to the idea that Jews were not loved by everyone. One afternoon, my ten-year-old sister Fran came home in tears because the playground bully called her a "dirty Jew." My mother sat my sister down, opened the Horace Mann School directory, looked up the kid's phone number, and dialed his home. The veins in her neck popped out, and her face turned red as she screamed, "Mrs. C., Hitler is dead!," at the bully's mother.

Helene Steinberg lived through the Nazi purge of European Jewry in the Paris apartment of her Catholic friend, Mary Louise Waldberger. Pupette, as she was called, was also hiding a Jewish husband, Raphael. Hitler's troops had distributed posters of what a "typical Jew" looked like so people would know what to watch for—a caricature with a long nose, heavy lips, and black, curly hair. Raphael, a dark, classic Sephardic Jew, was forced to stay off the streets.

Under Pupette's hand, the snub-nosed Helene Steinberg from Warsaw became Helene Moreaux, born in Algiers. She kept her yellow Star of David badge hidden in her drawer, and worked as an usher in a Parisian movie house. When she directed the Nazi soldiers to their seats she felt like kicking them, instead she smiled and made charming conversation. She would accompany Pupette to her Catholic church every week where the priests knew the truth but welcomed her anyway, even when she lined up for communion. Four days before the liberation of France, an informant told the police Helene Moreaux was a Jew. Two French security guards came to her door in Montmartre and ordered her to come with them. She cried: "Here's a knife. If you take me, you can take me dead." She fell on the floor and clutched their feet. "Maybe you have a daughter my age," she pleaded. The guards left the apartment.

As the teenage daughter of a perpetually grieving mother, I vowed to someday have children, lots of them, to replace the life in our family that was lost. I was always jealous of one of my best childhood friends, Patricia Hefner—she was one of twelve children, starting with Mary and ending with John. I barely had a dozen close relatives, period. But replenishing the bloodline was not a pressing priority. In the now, I wanted to have fun and explore and break free from a home where an ever present sadness made me feel old when I was young.

I went west to the University of Colorado in Boulder, and seeking the Rocky Mountain high that John Denver was touting I stopped eating meat, learned to ski, trained in yoga and Transcendental Meditation, and delved into the study of philosophy and Eastern religions. My goal was to unload the baggage in my brain and in my heart so I could be at one with the Vedic Cosmic Order. In the valley of the FlatIrons range, I yearned to be the peaks and the snow and the sky. Instead, at nineteen, I was usually twisted with anxiety and ambition, programmed by European parents since nursery school to pursue and achieve and win, American-style. Many weekend nights, as my new college girlfriends got stoned and glommed onto hunky mountain men, I would end up in my dorm room alone, morose over the superficial nature of youthful existence.

There are stacks of yellowed books on my office shelves from this era of alienation, books I devoured for strength, for peace. I read at night, and read in the morning, trying desperately to be at one with the river of joy and godliness—this, in part, as a distraction from the carnage going on in Vietnam, having been steeped in enough war stories for a lifetime. A sample of my seventies bibles includes *Zen Mind, Beginner's Mind* by Shunryu Suzuki, Soren Kierkegaard's *The Sickness Unto Death*, Krishnamurti's *Freedom from the Known*, and *Be Here Now*, by Baba Ram Dass, my favorite of all.

Here is an underlined passage from Krishnamurti that struck me at the time as crucial in my journey to transcend meaninglessness to Truth:

> *We are all confused about our many problems and lost in that confusion. Now, if one is lost in a wood, what is the first thing one does? One stops, doesn't one? One stops and looks round. But the more we are confused and lost in life the more we chase around, searching, asking, demanding, begging. So the first thing, if I may suggest it, is that you completely stop inwardly. And when you do stop inwardly, psychologically, your mind becomes very peaceful, very clear.*

Oh, God, how I wanted to know this stuff, to stop and be centered, to flow with the Now. I read Ram Dass's *Be Here Now* until the pages fell out, as I worked toward his "calming, centering, centering, calming, extracting myself from the drama." And enlightenment did come, but it would dance around me teasingly, then swiftly glide away. Most of the time I was another Ram Dass description, "like a yo-yo, I keep going up and coming down, up down, down, up, down." My friends were oscillating, too. Sam used to take three Quaaludes, listen to the wails of Jackson Browne, and sob like a baby. His girlfriend, Joy, would sit next to him on the couch, eyes closed, massaging her colon to rid her system of toxins, and open her soul.

What I saw in the mirror and at parties and in classes was wayward youth desperate to be anything else but what we were born into, middle-class suburbia. We wanted to be fascinating, elevated from ordinary life. So we meditated and hallucinated and took Jeeps deep into the mountains to Find Ourselves, whatever that meant. And when we came home from college on holiday breaks talking about cosmic dreams, our mothers and fathers would stare at their progeny with dread and fright.

It's no wonder, really. Most of our parents never had the time or the finances to be able to sit around and ponder the nature of existence, or to tap into Divine Energy sources. Growing up in the Depression, they were consumed with more earthly thoughts that had a lot more to do with Being Here Now than we would ever know, like figuring out how to pay for food and clothing. They weren't struggling over "Who Am I?" They were struggling just to get by. Memories of their impoverished pasts made them toil ruthlessly at jobs in order to raise well-dressed, well-schooled children who would feel safe and secure. So what did we do? We escaped from their safety nets as soon as we could, chasing danger and turbulence, dressed in faded army fatigues and Depression-era dresses purchased for pennies at used-clothing stores.

Predictability and mediocrity and materialism were not enough. We yearned to be bombarded by otherworldly sensations and bizarre experiences, the weirder the hit, the better it felt. We wanted to be exotic and hip and, most important, to be entertained. The Me Generation was starting up.

TAKE ME, CALIFORNIA

My own search accelerated in a big way after transferring to Stanford University, when the Bay Area was thick with reefer smoke, an exploding human potential movement, and aging hippies swathed in India-prints and African bead chokers strung on leather. I lived for a while in Synergy House, a depository for those desiring an "alternative lifestyle," the theme of the residence on the hill where we made our own granola in a kitchen swarming with flies and had weekly meetings to vote on things like whether to boycott grapes. I discovered the music of Eric Clapton and a tall, smart anthropology major from Pasadena who played a 1956 sunburst yellow Fender bass guitar and drove a 1969 white Ford Supervan, outfitted with an Oriental rug, Jimi Hendrix posters, and a mattress on the floor covered with batik fabric. When I first laid eyes on C.T. at a party where his band was playing, "he zonked me with his halfsmile and amour came surging" I told my diary. Amour continued to surge, in pain as much as passion, for the decade or so that we carried on, ending and mending our relationship.

In between an obsessive love and pursuing a joint degree in journalism and photography, I waitressed at the Varsity Theatre in downtown Palo Alto. This movie house circa 1927 featured vintage films like *Casablanca* and gourmet health food that helped pioneer what is now called the New American Cuisine. Flashing on those wonder years spent serving ratatouille and seafood crepes in a halter top and flowered skirt remind me of some of the most baffling and sexiest times of my life. Stanford in the mid-1970s was definitely more carnal and emotional than academic. Everything was steamy—my heart, the weather, the prism of culture refracting out of San Francisco colored by locals the Grateful Dead and Jefferson Airplane.

While the California landscape was lush and placid, my innards were tumultuous. My identity shifted with the semesters, with the ever changing Bay Area trends. In my quest to make sense of who I was, I was hypnotized. I was wired for biofeedback. I ate only brown rice, raw cashews, and Red Zinger tea for a week. I thrashed alone in the cold, gray ocean at Half Moon Bay. I sat in a lotus position for hours near the cliffs of Big Sur. Reaching toward nature for clarity, I became more muddled than ever. As I recorded in my journal in October 1974 after Big Sur: "I have become part of it all. I stood on the beach and the mountains melted into the ocean melted into the sand melted into me. I lost myself and found infinity." When I found myself again I would feel disjointed and alone.

By this stage, my natural curls were short and sprung free, inspired by the Afro worn by Angela Davis, who lectured to my Women in Mass Communication class. She had an amazing and indelible presence, head jutted forward, huge hair, huge earrings, huge voice. When she told us "The women's movement is more powerful than anything else today," I felt lucky to be young and female.

Yet I did not consider myself a militant feminist in 1974; the hardest part of the struggle toward equality had already been won, and we were coasting on its victory. Coming of age on authors like Simone de Beauvoir and Germaine Greer, never did I doubt that I could be anything I wanted to be. We were already more than a decade beyond the publication of Betty Friedan's *The Feminine Mystique*, the book that ignited the modern feminist movement by spurring young women to avoid the "trapped housewife" syndrome and heed the voices within that cried: "I want something more than my husband and my children and my home."

As the 1970s were upon us and *Ms.* magazine made its debut, women were already living those words, not fighting to make them true. In fact, being a woman was now about the coolest thing you could be. I thought of my own mother, the wife of a successful businessman, the wife of a community leader, forever Mrs. Theodore J. Krasnow. It was a rare letter that arrived addressed to her as Helene Krasnow; her identity was defined by the looming presence of my father, who I maybe twice saw bring his dishes from the dinner table and put them in the sink. He was a doting father who taught his kids to grab their dreams, but he was of the generation that thought housework was a female thing, a wife thing.

The sharpest memory I have of my mother as she shuffled my brother, sister, and me off to Horace Mann elementary school was as I looked over my shoulder, she would sigh deeply and sit down at the kitchen table where her place was marked with a black ashtray studded with fake turquoise, a book of crossword puzzles, and her knitting. And there she would remain for most of the morning, wearing black stretch pants, a flowered apron, and a striped kitchen towel over one shoulder, solving crosswords, making sweaters, and smoking Kent cigarettes. She did go out, grocery shopping, to her book club, to PTA meetings, to Hadassah functions, to play Scrabble with Shirley down the street. But when we came home she was always there and lunch was always on the table. School got out at 3 P.M., and after we walked the five minutes it took to get to the house, my mother would be waiting for us at the door. I knew she loved us but she rarely looked happy.

I discovered much later that she, indeed, felt trapped in that kitchen of the 1960s, but being a housewife at that time was what most women her age were doing. There were no girlfriends leading enticing, exciting lives to keep up with; her best friends were all at home, too. Surrounded by hard-charging Stanford women, I often thought of my mom at the Formica table in our pine-paneled kitchen in the Midwest with her glum expression and soft packs of Kents. The books that were making an impact on me inflamed my anger over the oppression of wives as a whole, and especially over my own mother, who was sharp and organized and could have been somebody big.

French writer Simone de Beauvoir calls women like my mother a "maniac housekeeper," and in *The Second Sex*, her 1949 frontrunner to modern feminist literature, paints domesticity this way:

> *The maniac housekeeper wages her furious war against dirt, blaming life itself for the rubbish all living growth entails. When any living being enters her house, her eye gleams with a wicked light: "Wipe your feet, don't tear the place apart, leave that alone!"*
>
> *In this insanity the house becomes so neat and clean than one hardly dares live in it; the woman is so busy she forgets her own existence. A household, in fact, with its meticulous and limitless tasks, permits a woman a sadomasochistic flight from herself as she contends madly with the things around her.*

I pictured my own girlhood home with its plastic runners on the carpet, and plastic covers on the couches and chairs in the living room. We did not wear shoes indoors, and frequently in the summer my mom would make us strip off our muddy clothes before entering. She viewed dirt as an evil invader into her home, her kingdom, the only sphere in her life she totally controlled. Reading Beauvoir I started to equate marriage with the death of dreams, a societally imposed force that snuffs the creative fires out of the female species. My mother had a beautiful voice and used to sing on the radio in Paris. She would have loved to have trained for the stage. So what was she doing with that contralto instead? Belting out French love songs while she did the ironing. This passage, highlighted in my old paperback copy of *The Second Sex*, cinched those sentiments:

> *The tragedy of marriage is not that it fails to assure woman the promised happiness—there is no such thing as assurance in regard to happiness—but that it mutilates her; it dooms her to repetition and routine... bound permanently to a man, a child in her arms, she stands with her life virtually finished forever. Real activities, real work, are the prerogative of her man: she has mere things to occupy her which are sometimes tiring, but never satisfying.*

I imagined myself someday in an elegant office, a master in business, not a slave to my home. I would never be this castrated character in Germaine Greer's *The Female Eunuch*: "While momma gorilla is breeding and nursing, poppa gorilla mounts guard over her, defending her from the perils of the wild." I would be right in the throes of the perilous wild with my pack of Stanford tigresses, Amy, Margie, Sarah, Linda, Parry, and Sandy. Revved by feminism and racy love, our prowess would not be, could never be, stopped. We were determined to be different from every generation of women that came before us, smarter, stronger, better.

There were plenty of distractions on the Bay Area playground taking us away from the call of traditional female instincts for order and procreation. As the first generation to be tantalized by the zipless sex in Erica Jong's 1975 book *Fear of Flying*, we slept with too many men, men we did not marry, men we did not love, men we did not even like that much. In the era that birthed shacking up and open marriage and effective, accessible birth control, sex was recreational, sex was mindless, sex was fun—or so we thought at the time. What we didn't know way back then was that the variety and voracity of our lusty recreation would later impair our ability to recognize truth in a relationship and make a commitment. But, hey, how about that Zipless when it first burst onto the scene? It paved the way for man after man, some chiseled idiots, others brilliant and rugged, still others just mistakes after too many strawberry daiquiris.

Here is one lusty Erica Jong description that fired curiosity in young women about short, anonymous encounters:

"Zipless because when you came together zippers fell away like rose petals, underwear blew off in one breath like dandelion fluff . . . Your whole soul flowed out through your tongue and into the mouth of your lover."

Yet it didn't take long for the Jerry Garcia fantasy that you could "Keep on Truckin' " recklessly to be thwarted by a sobering head-on with reality—too many choices spawned by women's liberation and the sexual revolution and the quest for Cosmic Consciousness had me reeling. It was a rough ride from teen to woman with wranglers like Germaine Greer and Erica Jong leading the way. At times I felt envy for my mother's generation, who often lost their virginity on their 1950s honeymoons in the Poconos and who flexed their brains by running PTAs. These mothers could have been running countries but instead they were at home running us. We turned out too ambitious and too adventurous.

When *Fear of Flying* was rendering us sexually fearless and completely confused, there was no AIDS to fear, just plenty of hard bodies and California beaches to loll around on. Along with the ability to sleep with anyone you found attractive came boundless freedom to pursue any career that appealed to you. My girl-friends were on their way to becoming lawyers, doctors, and M.B.A.s. Women could now do anything—a major problem for me. How could I become a career when I had yet to become a Self? This I did know: I loved to write and I was enchanted with celebrities, how they plotted their ascent, what fame felt like, if being revered by millions could ultimately make you happy.

That I would eventually become a journalist who specialized in profiling famous people probably had its origin sometime in the long night I spent with Erica Jong and entourage while she was visiting Stanford to give a lecture. I approached the author with a question and a press agent traveling with her invited me to join him and Jong and her then boyfriend at a local French restaurant. So I went and we drank too much red wine and my hero Erica Jong talked a lot about worries and loves and literature. It was easy to draw her out; it felt like what I was meant to do. When they dropped me off at Synergy House, I asked Jong and companions to come in and see the place. I was so proud when they sampled the homemade granola, our tribal food; thrilled to show them the coed bathroom window we crawled out of to stand on the roof where we sunbathed topless and grew herbs. They thought Synergy House was very cool.

As perplexing as it was, I, too, was enamored with this way-cool life on the outskirts of San Francisco in 1975, its perennially hip and sensual quality; the lazy, open-ended days. One surreal afternoon forever branded in my mind is the one spent with my soul brother John—John with the transparent blue eyes who dropped out senior year and moved to Mendocino, where he made furniture and fished for abalone. One Wednesday in the spring we romped through Muir Woods, home to towering redwoods and the most delicious damp forest smell, then moved on to the Alta Mira Hotel in Sausalito, where we drank ourselves silly on beer.

John's ponytail hung to the middle of his torn black T-shirt, his beard was wet with beer foam and speckled with tobacco from his nonfiltered Camels. My feet were propped on the railing of the balcony overlooking the Pacific Ocean, and I remember noticing how my leg hair flickered platinum in the sun and how wonderful my toes looked framed by purple velvet flip-flops with bamboo soles. Oak Park, Illinois, seemed like another planet. Here I was living with my surfer guitar-playing boyfriend, loving John who was living with someone else who once was the lover of the man I was living with, drunk in Sausalito, gazing lovingly at my feet.

I came back to Synergy, lay on the roof and thought about the molting and metamorphosis of caterpillars, the shedding of old bodies that kept them close to the ground and becoming something high-flying and free. That's what I felt was happening to me—"a change of physical form, structure, or substance, by supernatural means," as metamorphosis is defined.

My girlfriends were making their own striking transformations. Margie Eagan was a former high school cheerleader from Fall River, Massachusetts, a bleak, blue-collar mill town fifty miles south of Boston. Her father was a salesman for the Firestone Tire & Rubber Company, and every Sunday the Eagans, staunch Irish Catholics, went to church and sat in the same order in the same pew. Before arriving at Stanford in the fall of 1974, Margie had done two years at Smith College, the all-women's bastion of East Coast tradition where her big sister had gone. She was lured to the opposite coast by her favorite Joni Mitchell song: "Will you take me as I am . . . My heart cries out to you, California."

California took her as she was and turned Margie Eagan from Fall River and Smith and Irish immigrant grandparents into a surfing groupie with sun-bleached hair to her waist who used to meditate back-to-back with her Hawaiian boyfriend each morning at 6 A.M. before they hit the waves. They chose that meditation position so they could share the karma undulating up their spines.

For the better part of a year, Margie was enthralled with Bob from Maui and his wood-paneled station wagon like the model the Beach Boys used to bomb around in. She would tell us how at dawn they drove up and down Highway 1, along the Pacific Ocean, looking for what Bob would call "the most righteous swells." And as her boyfriend showed off his expert surfing skills, Marjorie, a straight-A student who believed herself to be a liberated woman, sat on the beach watching her guy reveling in his sport in a black rubber suit.

"I loved him because he epitomized everything enticing about California, everything different from what I had known back east," Margie explained. "He had gold flecks in his hair, for Chrissakes. He wore puka shells and Hawaiian shirts and drawstring pants. He was tan all over his body, even on his rear end. I wanted to be like him. I wanted to be everything that I wasn't."

We weren't the first generation of college-bound kids bent on busting loose like butterflies from parental-prescribed roles and constricting family cocoons. Wanting to be everything that you aren't, as Margie expressed, is what being young is about. Yet, with the mighty combination of new drugs, dissent against an old, nasty war, and pervasive cultural commands to march to our own beats, we were arguably better at goading the establishment than any youth block in history, shrillest in our cries "I Gotta Be Me."

While the Roaring Twenties toppled uptight Victorian mores with booze, cigarettes, flapper dress, sexual escapades, and the suffrage fight that awarded voting rights to women, the generation gap that widened after the mid-1960s ignited an uproar that reverberated in every layer of America. In her book on the evolution of the American family, *Embattled Paradise*, psychologist Arlene Skolnick describes the impact of the era this way: "An exhilarating and bewildering laboratory of social movements and experiments bubbled up around us and across the continent: the New Left, feminism, communes, the sexual revolution, cohabitation, the gay movement, and the beginning of the divorce revolution."

I often found myself more bewildered than exhilarated.

While my California body was brown and healthy, my California heart was gnarled like the roots of a redwood. My boyfriend, C.T., and I fought constantly, and I wanted to marry him. Perhaps he could be the anchor to life I so desperately wished to find. He would tell me that attachments to people cannot ultimately make you happy, you must find happiness from within. I was ripe for the teachings of Werner Erhard, which my friend Kelly promised was the ticket to tranquillity.

So I signed up for est, the Erhard Seminar Training, when the movement was just beginning to take hold in northern California. Unlike the seminars packed with hundreds that became the norm in later years, my training at the Jack Tarr Hotel in San Francisco consisted of twenty-two students. The simplicity of the est pitch sucked me in—that you could go from being a sad fool to the maker of your own destiny by creating the space to make your life work, completing your relationships, and extracting yourself from your sorry belief system. After ditching all this baggage, total transformation could be yours.

Werner Erhard had piercing eyes and a vein in his forehead that pulsated when he took the microphone; it was easy to fall into the magnetic field of the father of est, whose voice thundered and cracked. When he told us "the purpose of est is to rehabilitate your ability to experience," you believed that this was the one attendant in the vast spiritual fill-up station of the seventies who could tune your heart, fill your soul.

Erhard's message was a repackaged spiel from a long line

of other self-help salesmen that included Dale Carnegie and Norman Vincent Peale. To appeal to jaded psychowarriors of the seventies, Erhard updated his methods with mind-emptying techniques from Buddhism and terminology from the book *I'm OK, You're OK*. But in the case of est, it was more like I'm An Ass and So Are You. By 1974, some 65,000 people had bit. It was not surprising. The prospect of learning how to dissolve the barriers in your life to "make things go right, have them turn out perfectly, expand aliveness"—this from an est brochure—for $250 in a mere two weekends seemed to be a bargain.

At the end of est we were led through a series of exercises meant to connect us with our inner child, although the term had yet to come into vogue. The finale was a bunch of grown-ups sprawled across the carpet of the hotel ballroom, kicking, sobbing, shrieking, laughing, punching the air with our fists. The goal was to prove that you weren't the only loser in the world; everyone else was also a pathetic fool.

"Leave your crappy acts in here" were our est trainer's parting words.

When est ended I felt positively blissful, in sync with all mankind. So the planet was teeming with other crazies; this was absolutely wonderful news. I tackled my life with fresh zeal, completing my relationship with my parents by telling them I was living with my boyfriend, and completing my relationship with my boyfriend by telling him I no longer wanted to live with him. In the world according to Werner Erhard, completing a relationship means you come clean about everything.

The Great est Breakthrough lasted for about three months, until the old me came back, the sixth-grade spelling bee champion wired to reach and win and worry about everything. I was as sinewy as any California girl, but my soul had not been filled, not by Werner Erhard, not by Transcendental Meditation, not by thrusting my face to heaven on top of Mount Tamalpais. As hard as I had tried to grasp the egolessness of Zen and the Ram

Dass moment and the hush of nature, "I y'am what I y'am," as Popeye would say. And at the root of that person was an ego that needed to achieve tangible rewards.

I was also clear about something else, as I had been since I was a child who said her prayers diligently each night: There was a God, and I needed to get closer to Him or Her. My good friend Sarah, an ardent believer, helped fuel my desire to know the Lord. As a child growing up Episcopalian outside of Los Angeles, she had discovered church to be a refuge, a place where she always felt calm and, as she put it, "completely loved." While the norm at Stanford was to push toward a prestigious and powerful career, Sarah would tell me that all she felt compelled to do with her life was to be a loving person, and that this came from God.

Sarah was serene about the future, even though she had no firm professional goals—this when graduation was three months away. The rest of us, who knew exactly what fields we wanted to enter, were in knots. Her unflinching faith made me bent on traveling whatever path necessary to make my own treaty with God and to find my own spiritual peace.

It was anything but peace I would feel those first months out of college, when I chose to remain in Palo Alto, close to C.T., and keep my waitressing job at the New Varsity. John and his girlfriend, Susie, were killed in a head-on car crash driving from Colorado to California. These two friends, who had been everywhere, dancing like birds at campus parties, were gone forever. When these first friends I ever lost to death were buried, the layer that separated childhood from womanhood exploded into fragments. Everything else was changing, too. Amy had been accepted at a law school in Washington, Linda to medical school in Southern California, Margie got hired by a newspaper in Vermont. And Sarah was headed to Mother Teresa's convent in the South Bronx, with hopes of converting to Catholicism and becoming a nun. It was time to make my own move. "Kick door," my father urged me, as he always did when ～ about a big decision.

ɔ clear directives from the heart, the decision got made for me by circumstances. My father was diagnosed with kidney cancer, and in the span of two hours, I threw three years of my California life into a suitcase, got on a plane, and moved back to my hometown. It was February 1977, a brutally cold month that quickly slapped balmy Palo Alto out of me. My fifty-nine-year-old father had his right kidney removed, and the reports after surgery showed the cancer had been confined to that organ. He required no radiation or chemotherapy. That night on my knees next to my childhood bed my God was as real as Sarah's God as I said my Thank Yous for saving Theodore Krasnow. Tears soaked my old orange bedspread, and I was overcome with the realization that the parents I assumed were mine forever were also part of the fragile and fleeting universe.

HOT, HAPPENING, ALIVE!

I shaved my legs, grew my nails, bought a navy blue suit at Bonwit Teller, and interviewed for jobs. After six months at a dreary public relations firm, I joined another agency that spangled with life, one that handled the publicity for Broadway shows, rock concerts, fashion designers, and the best restaurants in town. Everything new and hot that opened in the city was launched by Margie Korshak & Associates in the John Hancock Tower, a firm that still reigns supreme as the glitz machine of Chicago. When you entered our thirtieth-floor suite overlooking Lake Michigan, the first sight was a neon sign that spelled out "Margie" in hot pink and purple neon. You never knew who might be roaming our halls, one day Joel Grey, the next Sammy Davis, Jr. Standing outside Margie's office, you could hear her on the telephone cajoling stars like Yul Brynner and Henry Fonda and Liza Minnelli.

These were years spent squiring celebrities around Michigan Avenue in purple cowboy boots and an ankle-grazing possum coat. Years spent with two-inch red nails and henna highlights, hungry to be the top producer of the firm, to have the city at my feet. I remember my first limousine ride—when I was assigned to be Sugar Ray Leonard's escort to a round of television and radio shows, and to an appearance at an inner-city school. There I was next to this gorgeous prizefighter in the backseat of a black stretch Cadillac, clad in fur and chatting away about mundane stuff like the great season the Chicago Bears were having.

This was as *Cosmo* magazine as you could get, limo ride alone with a famous, spectacular-looking guy. I fantasized what it would be like if he tried to kiss me. Attempting to bring it on, I threw my head back and closed my eyes. Sugar Ray did not get my cue. He stayed close to the window on his side of the seat and continued to talk about Bear running back Walter Payton.

The only time a star did kiss me the whole five years I worked for Margie Korshak was Henny Youngman, who was then in his mid-seventies and doing a New Year's Eve act at a nightclub our firm represented. In fact, old Henny tried to kiss me a lot that night.

There were no more picnics on sun-drenched California hills with bean sprouts and cream cheese slabbed between sunflower seed bread. A typical lunch was now a Cobb Salad and cold Crème Senegalaise soup at the dark and clubby Cricket's restaurant. In just a few months, I went from gypsy of the forest to urban chick. Reflecting on the transition, I am not surprised at how effortlessly I fell into this new character. After the wrenching inward journey in California, I was gleeful to be Out There in Chicago, networking nightly at Riccardo's, the city's notorious hangout for journalists located near the *Chicago Sun-Times,* the *Chicago Tribune,* and *Chicago* magazine.

The dream job at Margie Korshak with my head in the stars and packed social life enveloped me safely in a cushion of frivolity. My columnist friend Roger Simon called me "Chicago's Director of Fun." The icon of the times, *Saturday Night Fever,* was thumping for me every day of the week. I was proudly, ecstatically, one of "Margie's Poodles," or so we were described in a story on Margie Korshak by *Chicago Sun-Times* reporter Rick Kogan that appeared on the cover of the Sunday magazine in February 1979. The article, titled "The Princess of Pizzazz," featured a full-blown head shot by celebrity photographer Victor Skrebneski of Margie, then forty. Margie with the mane of silver hair and floor-length Fendi mink trimmed with fox and her stable of loyal poodles. We would do anything for her, and she knew it. As she told Kogan, who wrote a column called "Dr. Nightlife": "My girls would kill for me." And when he interviewed me about Margie, this is what I had to say at the awestruck age of twenty-four: "I've never been the kind of person who liked to be in anyone's shadow. But with Margie I haven't minded at all. She has an incredible, incredible shadow. I could stay there forever."

However gushing, I meant every word. I loved Margie; after my first year there she gave me and her assistant Janie Goldberg diamond pavé rings. By securing a spot in her towering shadow, we were ushered into an amazing galaxy. One of the accounts I supervised, Jam Productions, booked and staged most of the rock concerts, comedians, and solo acts that played Chicago. The majority of the performances took place at Park West, a nightclub/pickup hub packed with Chicago's most eligible men.

I would sit at Park West's horseshoe bar several nights a

week while I took in acts like Bruce Springsteen, Gilda Radner, Joan Baez, Elvis Costello, Talking Heads, Isaac Hayes, Stanley Turrentine, Emmylou Harris, and the Police. In addition to attending shows, my job also entailed taking some of these people to media interviews. When I met Steve Allen at O'Hare Airport his plane had arrived thirty minutes late. We were expected at a radio show, so we had to sprint down the airport corridor to the limousine, and speed down the expressway to downtown Chicago.

I was thrilled to be racing down the corridors of O'Hare flanked by Steve Allen. People whispered, pointed, wondered who I was. Granted, Steve Allen was an aging comic who had his hair sprayed into a pompadour—I mean, this was not Iris and Mick Jagger—but my ego was still bursting. After all, he was A Star.

The night of the Steve Allen performance at Park West was a landmark in my evolution. As I watched him do his timeless schtick, Chicago's Director of Fun was starting to get winces of discontent. What was I doing? Who was I? The onetime spiritual voyager on a quest for Cosmic Consciousness and God was turning into a celebrity sponge. The existential wince turned into a sharp pain when I approached my new best friend Steve Allen backstage and he gave me a look like he had never met me before in his life. I reminded him that I was the girl who had picked him up at the airport, and he gave me a mechanical smile. That distant smile crushed me and enlightened me.

Here's the deal with show business: You may believe the stars you spend long hours with become your friends. They are not your friends. During the course of intimate hours alone, they may tell you of broken romances, wayward children, a drug habit kicked long ago. You will share a few personal, juicy details in return. But that is generally The End of the Relationship. It is a flicker of a relationship, a fleeting moment that doesn't matter.

So what does matter?

I still felt as torn as the eighteen-year-old freshman in Boulder who read Victor Frankl's *Man's Search for Meaning* while her roommate was passed out on her bed from too many bongs off a Lucite Tokemaster. How did having everything in Chicago end up feeling like nothing? Park West wasn't doing it for me. The men who wanted me I couldn't stand, and the men I wanted most were hurting me. I was jaded, wounded, numb to love. It was like eating a whole box of chocolates; after a while every nougat tasted the same, the caramels, the syrupy cherries, the vanilla cremes.

Late at night in my apartment in Lincoln Park, across from the zoo, I could hear drunken yelps from Ichabod's, the singles' bar next door, and be overcome by loneliness. My closest girl-friends from Chicago—Ellyn, Janie, and Debbie—were married, as was my Palo Alto sister Sarah. My Boulder buddies, Simone and Josette, were engaged. I had already been a bridesmaid three times. I loved Margie Korshak, but I started to hate my glamorous life.

One client, The Fairfax Hotel, was based in Washington, D.C., and during a business trip I met an attorney there who spun my head around. He was thirty-four and had never been married and lived in a white stucco house with a white picket fence. He also had a law degree from Harvard and an art collection that ranged from Frank Stella to Robert Rauschenberg. Phew—he was everything, my fantasy man in my fantasy city.

The first time he took me to his house with the daffodils and irises and a hammock in the backyard, I felt that what I wanted more than anything else was to hunker down with one man, have his children, and watch them run around a yard filled with flowers. But instead, at the age of twenty-five, I was flitting around Chicago with red fingernails, clutching a champagne flute at Arnie's, Riccardo's, Tango, The Pump Room, Otto's. I was everywhere; I was nowhere.

As the Washington lawyer and I dated over a six-month stretch, I became convinced that he was The One who would tame the Cosmo Girl into the wife and mother she was meant to be. What I didn't know at the time I was falling hard for the man with the incredible Oriental rugs was that he was simultaneously falling hard for two other women. After I gave him a red silk shirt for Valentine's Day he told me that, although he could see spending the rest of his life with me, it wasn't quite time to start the rest of his life.

And so it was with me as it was with all of my single and liberated and successful friends, we'd get dumped or we'd dump but then we'd get right back on the horse. For all our accomplishments in professional pursuits, this Stone Age truth was still running us: Woman wants to find her Prince. During one bruised-heart period, I went on a two-week healing vacation to a Club Med in Morocco, and on the airplane home from Marrakech drank tiny bottles of Chenin Blanc and mourned dreams dashed, loves lost, the Washington lawyer, my high school honey, and beautiful C.T. of California, who was still lingering. I cried for the lack of permanence all around me. Didn't anything last?

The surface rhythm of my life kept me distracted—manicures on Mondays, morning runs along the lakefront, a different restaurant or concert every night. But the truth about a frenzied life that is built on being Out There is that on those rare moments when you stop and focus In There, you crash. After the picket fence epiphany in Washington, I now looked at the mothers pushing strollers along Oak Street Beach with envy. These women had the real stuff of life. I wanted the real stuff, not to be running on empty in the white-hot, fastest lane. I wanted a husband, not this list of has-beens in my diary. I wanted to be Grounded in Truth, not to be feeling like that high school cheerleader grinning hugely and acting out a life that wasn't really hers.

During my years at Korshak I had been freelancing features to the *Chicago Tribune* and profiles to *Chicago* magazine. As I become more experienced as a reporter, I decided to change careers. In public relations you are in the business of fostering images; as a journalist you try to extract the essence of people. That's the spot I wanted to be in. An exhaustive profile I did on Chicago real estate magnate Arthur Rubloff generated some controversy and got the attention of the features editor of the *Dallas Times Herald*. He flew me down to Texas and said: "We have two beats open. You can be the fashion writer or you can be the rock critic." I chose fashion.

When I arrived at the Dallas–Fort Worth Airport to look for an apartment, I was met by a soft-spoken, big-spending Texan named Bruce who had baby blue eyes, a matching Mercedes, and worked for one of my Chicago clients. Bruce was the quintessential Dallas entrepreneur: a real estate magnate; owned part of an airline, a hotel, and a furniture company; and was dating a Playboy bunny. Before we went house-hunting, he pulled into the parking lot of a store in North Dallas called the Western Warehouse that took up half a city block. "If you're moving to Texas, you have to own a pair of real Texas cowboy boots," he told me.

We left the Western Warehouse with a $325 pair of lizard boots the color of Bordeaux wine, sexy stompers with three-inch heels and interlocking gold horseshoes on the tops. That was my welcome to Texas. And those lizard boots stamped with the lucky horseshoes of gold became a symbol of the next three years. For what I found behind that door I kicked open in Texas made the glitz of Chicago seem like flimsy tinsel. The flash and excess that defined Ronald Reagan's feel-good eighties all came together in Texas, rich on an oil industry that had been shifted back to the States after the Arab OPEC crisis.

Everything sparkled in Dallas, Texas—the mirrored buildings, the sequined gowns, the diamonds as big as pecans, the frosty-blond poufs. With Bruce I learned the Texas Two-Step at Billy Bob's in Fort Worth, the world's largest honky-tonk that holds up to six thousand people, saw Willie Nelson, and attended the Cattle Baron's Ball where I first heard the expression "He's richer than God." Before long I had a slight drawl. The pangs to be a homebody with a lawyer husband in a backyard of babies had totally, miraculously, disappeared. My career was igniting and that overshadowed all else. As Dallas was peaking as a city, it attracted journalists from all over the country, a tight-knit circle of young, single transplants eager to tear things up.

It felt exactly like the earliest days of Margie Korshak Associates. Hot. Happening. Alive! Although I was headquartered in the Deep South, top designers from New York, Rome, and Paris all made regular stops because one of their best accounts was based in Dallas, the retail giant Neiman Marcus. So I had the opportunity to interview a global cast of designers, a list that spanned Bill Blass, Oscar de la Renta, Perry Ellis, Carolina Herrera, Karl Lagerfeld, Gianni Versace, Paul Smith, and Todd Oldham—then a local teenage wunderkind doing quirky knits, today the king of crazy couture.

But reporting on fashion soon began to feel as if I were spooning out cotton candy—sugary, sheer mounds that melted on the tongue then were gone. Yet unlike past years when existential angst could put me in bed for days, in Dallas I kept on keeping on. I had to. Seasons were changin', and I had to quickly move on to the front lines of the new trends. Clothes did not matter, this I knew. But I was hooked. And as our Dallas days unfolded, so were my friends. Women and men. It was tough not to care about clothes; this was a city of fashion-stallions. Dallas was so dazzling that even the football players fell prey—the official Cowboys uniform included silver metallic trousers.

Along with some of those Dallas Cowboys, we spent many evenings writhing to Lionel Ritchie's "All Night Long" at

Nostromo, a club where the city's biggest real estate deals took place, as did the town's most illicit love affairs. In that club that smelled like Opium perfume, sweat, and old leather, I was distracted from my hungering heart, especially the night Hank showed up.

Hank was a traveling salesman from Brooklyn who came to town one week every season to sell his clothing at the Dallas Apparel Mart. He wore gray plastic glasses and he was shorter than me and he talked so fast and funny he sounded like a comic from the Catskills. But he had thick hair and the right lines and I fell for them and for him. He would go back to New York and I wouldn't hear from him until he came back to Dallas months later with trunkfuls of new dresses, and new excuses. When Hank appeared at Nostromo one spring with the woman he had been living with for the past eleven years I finally got the picture.

Other women in my group were also bent on turning their Mr. Wrongs into princes. We were used to achieving what we wanted in careers through perseverance, why shouldn't that work with men, too? It did not. To protect our souls and hearts of jelly, we tried to concoct hard and impenetrable outer shells. Following the lead of Jane Fonda, we became the female fitness hounds who put books like *How to Have Thinner Thighs in Thirty Days* in the best-selling category.

To be like the rippled bodies sprawled across the decks of Dallas swimming pools, I started lifting free weights. I did the Nautilus circuit three times a week. I jogged every morning at Kenneth Cooper's Aerobics Fitness Center. My new guru was Arnold Schwarzenegger. By going for the burn in my muscles, the burn in my heart was masked.

In the bars at night I felt hot, hotter, hottest—the turquoise jewelry against skin burnished russet by the Texas sun, the flouncy sundresses with no backs, muscled arms, no belly. Yet it was at this physical peak that I began to despise exercise and fashion. The books on firm thighs and tight buttocks were hardly feeding my spiritual abyss. I looked great but felt lousy. The toughest women in the gym all told me that strong bodies made you stronger in all tracks of your life. Yet if hardness led to happiness, why couldn't I sustain that high that came after a three-mile run? Something big was off.

Werner Erhard would have told me "Your life is not working."

And indeed, even after all these years of trying to get it right, puffing uphill in my career and in relationships, I was still running in place. I thought of Margie Eagan, my Stanford ally who had tried to find happiness by becoming something she wasn't. I, too, was, once again, becoming something I wasn't. My editor and close friend Kim Marcum, a fellow midwesterner, and I used to talk all the time about what we wanted and what we had and why the two didn't jive.

Kim was from St. Joseph, Missouri, a town of eighty thousand, wedged between the wheat fields of Kansas and the prairies of Nebraska. "It was a dullsville place of people settled into cul-de-sac lives," Kim would say. Dallas was a lot of things but it was never dull; purple-haired punks ran clothing stores, the Tex-Mex food was doused with fiery peppers, the country music sounded like ballads from the moon to us midwestern girls raised on rock and blues. And the crop of men we could pick from was plenty varied, from cowboys in pointy boots and silver belt buckles that shone like headlights to bankers in Armani suits with bulging Coach wallets. Everyone in Dallas was an entrepreneur, no one cranked away at the same job for thirty and forty years like our relatives back in Kansas City and Chicago. But the kaleidoscopic trends and people lurching at Kim and me from all directions made us miss the steadying, dullsville towns we had fled.

As the wild child again started caving in to the woman who desired stability, I stretched the boundaries of my beat into subjects such as maternity and wedding attire. Marriage was heavy on my mind. Ann Zimmerman, a Long Islander at the newspaper, had met Michael Gallant, a Dallas advertising executive, and it was obvious that he was The One. My sister, a lifelong best friend, had just announced that she and her husband, Seth, were expecting their first child. And Lady Diana had recently cascaded down the aisle in a fairy-tale ceremony that made it impossible to be single and female and not be wishing for your own Prince Charming. At twenty-eight, a longing for a baby had a grip on my womb and heart.

My friends at the paper with parallel lives were feeling as I felt, that it was time to put an end to the "musical chairs," as described by Ann Zimmerman. After years of rousing living as a journalist in Philadelphia, then Washington, D.C., she was more than ready to find the chair where she would finally land.

"What a relief to have met Michael," Zimmerman remembers. "After all these years I could finally stop auditioning for the part. I had been addicted to tumultuous, insane, bad relationships; they were like drugs. But the chase was intoxicating. Even though I knew Michael was the real thing, I fought it for a long time. Michael was so normal, I missed the excitement."

My next boyfriend, Timothy, seemed normal enough at first, but over a year and a half we would forge a union that turned out to be the strangest thing that ever happened to either one of us. Timothy was Swedish and owned an Arabian horse and was interested in everything: He could quote as liberally from the New Testament as he could from Jack Kerouac, liked tofu as well as barbecued ribs. His beat at the *Times Herald* was to rove the state and twang the Dallas consciousness with subjects like murder, poverty, racism, and God-fearing small-town Texas life. He taught Sunday school at a Presbyterian church and filled my ears with the gospel; I added a Willi Smith shirt and Alexander Julian tie to his closet full of Eddie Bauer.

I dropped out of the Nostromo scene and started wearing

my oldest clothes, those cozy rags from Palo Alto, as I fluffed my nest at home and wanted what I had, for a change, loving someone who loved me. An interview with Perry Ellis helped to propel me farther away from the dazzling Dallas scene. In the story titled "Seventh Avenue's Class Act," I traced the evolution of the then forty-three-year-old designer credited with pioneering the modern sportswear movement. His whimsical linens that grazed the ankle and his chopped-off cotton sweaters earned Ellis several Coty awards. But real happiness, he assured me, came from somewhere else.

"There's nothing real about fame for me," Ellis said in a near whisper. "Fortunately, I think the success I have in my life has very little to do with the public side of it. True success comes from personal relationships and the knowledge that something you do, you do very well. If the result of that is some kind of public recognition, then that's great.

"But there's nothing real about fame for me. You can't take that to bed with you, and you can't hold on to that. There's nothing there, it's empty. There are three areas of my life that are important to me. Matters of heart, my health, and my work."

After the article appeared he sent me a wild orchid plant with one white flower edged in purple. It was a gift of class, simple and austere, but it didn't live long. Neither did Perry Ellis; by the spring of 1986 he and his love, Laughlin Barker, were both gone, of AIDS.

From the session with Perry Ellis it became clear that I had to take my journalism beyond linen and peek-a-boo lace and the latest high-cut maillots sliced to the navel. "I mean, how many times can you write about swimsuits?" the *Dallas Times Herald*'s fashion editor Kim Marcum used to groan from the seat next to me. One afternoon I got a call out of nowhere from a woman named Andrea Herman who told me she had just been hired to start up a features department at United Press International's world headquarters in Washington, D.C. She asked me if I would be interested in covering national trends and famous people in the capital. It wasn't exactly the back-to-the-soul transition I'd been thinking of embarking on after Perry Ellis, but who could resist that plum?

When Max McCrohon, the editor in chief of UPI, telephoned me to officially offer me the position after a round of interviews, I listened openmouthed and heart atwitter as he described the new beat: "Princess Caroline of Monaco has been at the White House this week," McCrohon started out in his breathy Australian accent. "And it was a real shame, because we had no one at UPI to cover that event. That's the kind of stories you would be doing."

"Would my beat be limited to Washington?" I asked him.

He laughed. "No, Iris. What we have in mind for you is something more global."

For as long as I live I will remember the zing I felt all over when my new boss promised me "something more global" in my career. Here I had been sequestered in one southern city writing on a fluffy subject that had started to smother me, and now the world was truly mine, the universe. I forgot all about Texas and Timothy, who when I told him I had found a better job in another city told me that was fine, because he had found Jesus Christ. I forgot all about domesticity and said yes to UPI, the adrenaline from the chase still surging in my veins.

THE CHAOS

➤ ◄

I began at United Press International on March 1, 1984, feeling very happy and very global. But my first day quickly began to unravel. After years of sun-splashed Texas dappled with beautiful people, I felt as if I had landed in the tunnels of hell. The blinds in our suite of offices were all pulled shut so there was no light from the outdoors streaming in, the carpet was the color of burnt cobalt and splattered with coffee stains, and most of the natives were men with foul mouths and big bellies. This coarse newsroom was a prototype for what Hollywood attempts to re-create in movies about journalists, only this place was real and it was brutal to break into. Defiant and anachronistic in the age of CNN, UPI is one of those bastions of journalism where reporters tend to stay for twenty and thirty years.

Many of these grizzled veterans had covered civil rights marches, the assassinations of the Kennedy brothers and Martin Luther King, the war in Vietnam. Walter Cronkite, David Brinkley, Eric Sevareid, and Howard K. Smith are UPI alumnae, and this history makes Unipressers—as the wire service's reporters call themselves—feisty and full of themselves and harshly serious about the news business. I can tell you the flash writer from Texas whose scariest frontline experience thus far had been fighting for a front-row seat at a Calvin Klein show was viewed as a hothouse flower that would quickly wilt.

But the gloom began to lift when Max McCrohon and Andrea Herman made good on their promises. They told me to make a list of ten people I wanted to interview anywhere in the world. UPI was starting a series called Lifesize, lengthy profiles of international celebrities in a broad range of professions, from the performing arts to politics, and I was to be a primary contributor to this section of our report. On the back of a paper napkin at Childe Harolde bar in DuPont Circle I wrote out the following wish list: Billy Graham, Ted Kennedy, Yoko Ono, Barbara Bush, Queen Noor of Jordan, Robert Rauschenberg, Wayne Newton, Elie Wiesel, Indira Gandhi, and Norman Mailer. When I left my job five years later, I had profiled eight of the ten. The two missing were Mrs. Gandhi, who someone else at UPI got to first in what turned out to be the prime minister's last print interview prior to her assassination, and Wayne Newton, who I lost interest in.

This was only the frosting. I would also have my byline on stacks of other stories on stars, from Famous-for-Fifteen-Minute types, such as Cyndi Lauper's hairdresser, to long-running legends like Ginger Rogers. During my first weeks at UPI I used to slink into the newsroom, eyes cast downward, to avoid the bristly natives. Now there was a bounce in my walk over to my computer terminal, where I would prop my Texas cowboy boots on the desk and start working the phone to see who I could get to.

I got to lots of them, including Elisabeth Kübler-Ross, Deepak Chopra, Dominick Dunne, Louise Nevelson, Germaine Greer, Werner Erhard, and Mr. Rogers. Meeting nearly anybody I wanted made me feel important; this was certainly a step up from fashion shows. Here I was on the front row of life. People at UPI started to be nicer to me; I gave them good gossip.

So more than a decade after Erica Jong first teased me about the complexity of fame, I was in a position to root around the psyches of celebrities for myself, to find out what drives them, what their parents were like, if fame was all it was cracked up to be, or if it was the empty vessel described by Perry Ellis. I would come to find out that celebrity-ism brings on as much unhappiness as it does happiness. Yet, those who get to the top share some common, significant traits.

They possess a vigor of the spirit and unrelenting tenacity, qualities as essential as talent for success. We fall under the spell of people who are capable of sticking with their passions of the soul without getting sidetracked by too much recognition or failure or by life itself. I think of the sovereign abstract expressionist painters who self-destructed as relatively young men. David Smith and Jackson Pollock killed themselves driving recklessly. Mark Rothko's paintings became blacker and blacker, then he slashed his wrists. But other artists who spun out of that movement, such as Willem de Kooning and Robert Rauschenberg, managed to paint through their demons and prevail, however tormented were their minds along the way. There is clearly much to learn from persons who persevere and go on to amass a grand body of work over time, often at immense personal cost. There is also much to learn from persons who burn out. As a psychojournalist I picked up some valuable life lessons on What Really Matters—the pivotal question of my life.

The actors, authors, artists, politicians, and New Age gurus I interviewed may have had little in common on the surface. Yet after many months into the celebrity shuffle it became obvious there were some key similarities among those who were the most content: they had a strong family structure; they were passionate, even altruistic, about their work; they were rooted in spiritual beliefs; and they weren't impressed by their own success. These four areas seemed to substantiate the ephemeral nature of fame.

When the conversation turned to God and family, some of the most formidable of subjects grew open and animated. Senator Ted Kennedy took off his black-lens sunglasses and his blue eyes sparkled as he shared how he's most content when sailing on his boat *Mya* with his kids, then coming back to the house in Hyannis Port to a big, roaring fire. I asked this man who receives on the average a thousand letters a day and serves as the father figure to an extended clan of twenty-eight nieces and nephews where he turns for his own strength:

"It comes through very basic factors," said Kennedy, staring into the distance. "The powers of memories of my brothers and sisters. I always loved them very much, and knew they loved me. They have been a very powerful inspiration for my whole life. Faith has also been very important. And there's an element of hope, which I find has been more of a strong factor guiding me in my own life than the issues of despair and cynicism.

"And although it's been challenged at different times, it's still my central force."

When I interviewed Kennedy, it was coming up on June 6, the anniversary of Robert Kennedy's assassination, and there had been numerous tributes and memorial services in RFK's honor. The one son of Joseph and Rose Kennedy who lived to turn gray said that waves of hero worship is missing the point of his fallen brothers' lives:

"I'm very proud of my name, and I'm very proud of what my brothers had been able to achieve," Kennedy started out. "But the fact remains that I knew what they were as people. And the last thing they wanted was to be viewed as heroes. They were very special individuals who had very special strengths, and they also had weaknesses. I know they felt that whatever was a part of the legacy belonged to everyone. And that legacy is that you didn't have to be a senator or be a president to make a difference. You just had to make a difference. They believed in a universal sense of caring and willingness to involve yourself in something for someone else. And that's how they would want to be remembered."

Along with profiles, in which I attempted to cut to the heart of a person, I also turned out a trend story nearly every week, article after article on the fickle lifestyles of the 1980s. I covered everything percolating in Yuppieland, from picking up dates at gourmet supermarkets to sperm banks specializing in genius-donor specimens. It got to a point that I couldn't stand to hear about anything trendy anymore, not risotto, not liposuction, not smart drugs, antioxidants, Australian merlot, Canyon Ranch, Donna Karan, or anything else Fabulous.

A decidedly unfabulous aspect of the frenetic eighties was squeezing in time for love, or failing to find it in the first place. Everyone wanted it—A Relationship—but no one seemed to have it, because we worked all the time and we expected our men to be as flawless as our wines. I developed a subspecialty on trends in yuppie love, chronicling the death of the sexual revolution, the return of monogamy, the burgeoning match-making industry, and the loneliness of being single.

Many of my interviews with the lovelorn stuck with me at night, haunting me while dining solo on Lean Cuisine fettuc-cine, slouched in the tattered, brown plaid chair my father bought me for $40 at Montgomery Ward the winter I moved to Chicago and got my first apartment. Back then it represented an object of independence, my own new chair, not the thrift-store junk from college, furnishing my own living room in sin-gle's central, Lincoln Park. Pushing thirty and living alone in Washington, D.C., that chair made me miserable.

Although we looked to books like Janice Harayda's *The Joy of Being Single* for reassurance and support, with its advice to "stop putting your life on hold and start living," it struck me that the only way I might be able to start really living was if I put this life on hold. Skinny, Single, and Successful was not a path to the Golden Light. So much for our claims of how won-derfully free we felt to have postponed the chains of marriage to Find Ourselves.

Granted, there were euphoric bursts to be had from self-discovery—Embassy Row parties, assignments in Paris, and a byline that shot around the globe. But the moments didn't amount to any lasting highs; having a Hot Career means you never savor where you are when you are there, because you are too consumed by the climb. Something huge was missing on a day-to-day basis, the serene knowing that my friend Sarah seemed to have back in Palo Alto that the Now was splendid in itself without scurrying up to the next summit to see if that view was better. Some balance came from volunteering Sunday afternoons at a nursing home and tutoring inner-city junior high kids in language skills. And that truly felt good, but that, too, wasn't enough. I wanted roots, thick and sprawled and enduring, and to stop feeling like a kite.

"You've come a long way, baby," the Virginia Slims ads had been promising since they first appeared in 1969, depicting old pictures of Women's Suffrage demonstrators. How far had we come? At what hallowed destination had we arrived if, rather than cooking spaghetti and meat sauce from scratch, we were carrying out cellophane noodles from gourmet supermarkets where we were also shopping for husbands? Here I was with press clearance to the White House and a great résumé, when all I really wanted was the marrow of life, the essence Henry David Thoreau speaks of in *Walden*.

We must learn to reawaken and keep ourselves awake, not by mechanical aids, but by an infinite expectation of the dawn . . . I went to the woods because I wished to live deliberately, to front only the essential facts of life, and see if I could not learn what it had to teach, and not, when I came to die, discover that I had not lived. I did not wish to live what was not life, living is so dear. I wanted to live deep and suck out all the marrow of life. . . .

Instead of sucking the marrow of life, we were grazing on cilantro and playing Trivial Pursuit. One-upping each other with superficial TV trivia kept us from having to reveal any of our raw innards, the pain deep inside. This Having It All stuff was a hoax; having everything was exactly like having nothing. Anyone who was honest would admit they were starving for emotional intimacy, for meaning beyond jaunts to Corfu, that we were desperate for babies to love.

I thought of my own little clique of reporters at UPI, people with whom I worked ten-hour days, and people with whom I drank after work to talk about the job. Work, work, work, work. Drunk and drained, I would return to my apartment around 9 P.M., then often telephone my parents in Chicago while nibbling take-out sushi. I'd have to drum up enthusiasm to resume discussion of my job—what stars I had met that week, what stars I would meet the next. I basked in their delight in their daughter, the international feature writer based in the capital of the United States. Yet usually, at the end of these conversations with crackly, long-distance voices I couldn't get enough of, I'd break down. I'd tell my mother and father I was getting sick of spending time with famous people I'd meet once and never see again, that I missed seeing and hugging my family.

My dad would then say to me: "Don't be sad. Tomorrow you start a new life."

Choked with tears, I'd tell him that tomorrow I would be back at UPI slamming away on the computer, writing about the stars.

He would then ask me, "Do you have any new boyfriends?" I couldn't tell him that I was still yearning for Born-Again Timothy, who was now enrolled in seminary. I'd laugh and say, "Dad, what do you want me to do? Get married, stay home, and have babies?" He always responded the same way: "That wouldn't be so bad."

It was in this angst over Christ's hold on Timothy that I

became very serious about having a head-on with God myself. I started spending less time at the bars with my UPI friends after work, instead flopping down on the couch with books on Jewish mysticism that had recharged me when I was a purveyor of glitz in Texas, like the thin paperback called *The First Step: A Guide for the New Jewish Spirit* by Alman Schacter-Shalomi with Donald Gropman. Schacter-Shalomi, a devotee of Buddhism as well as Born-Again Judaism, was my kind of rabbi; this was a man who referred to God as "Cosmic Majesty."

As he writes: "Our ability to connect with the universe is especially strong at dawn and dusk, sunrise and sunset. Whenever you can, spend that time walking your human being, walking your soul."

The idea of walking my soul socked me square in the heart. When was the last time I had even walked with my legs let alone my soul? Always squashed for time, I drove everywhere in a rush, or sped through Washington in a taxi to interviews in Georgetown and on Capitol Hill, then back to UPI to hammer out stories on deadline.

How exactly does one learn to Walk Your Soul after zooming around the material world for so long?

I started to attend Friday night services at Adas Israel, a large Conservative congregation on Connecticut Avenue in northwest Washington, where it was obvious by the packed sanctuary of young people seated around me that I wasn't the only spent fast-tracker who had landed on her knees. The gluttony of the eighties was giving way to a vast spiritual hunger, and Christian dating services and Jewish singles events were replacing bars as the venues to meet mates. My friends in the fields of finance and real estate who had been riveted to the biography of Chrysler king Lee Iacocca now couldn't get enough of *The Road Less Traveled*, M. Scott Peck's watershed book on grace and spiritual growth. Peck was telling us things like "Ultimately love is everything" and "In the communion of growing consciousness, of knowing with God, there is enough joy to sustain us." How soothing and simple these words resonated in a life that had gotten remote and complicated. Capitalists turned spiritualists became a big media story, especially in Washington, where fundamentalist leaders of the New Right such as Jerry Falwell and Pat Robertson were mobilizing voters with tirades on America's moral decay and the erosion of family values.

I happily embraced this latest trend in my work at UPI, even if it meant following the chilling proliferation of the Moral Majority and televangelism. During this era I sought out interviews with people like Chuck Colson, the former special counsel to President Nixon who wrote the best-selling *Born Again*, and evangelist Billy Graham.

In the course of my conversations with these hellfire Christians I struggled to learn more about my own relationship with God, and more about Timothy, who by this point was one changed man. My once amorous, left-wing, long-haired boyfriend had turned into a short-haired celibate. If it was indeed Jesus himself who was possessing Timothy, I had to understand the draw—after all, Jesus was Jewish.

Tracking God

For Charles Colson, the ex-special counsel to President Nixon who spent seven months in prison for his part in the Watergate break-in, a conversion to Christ was quick and explosive. This came after a classic yuppie career, years before the term *yuppie* was even coined. At the age of twenty-five, Colson was already an administrative assistant in the U.S. Senate, and by the age of thirty-nine, he was one of only a handful of people with direct access to the president of the United States. Then came the Watergate exposé, Nixon's resignation, and Colson's humiliating tumble. As a broken man at the bottom, he found what he considered a "greater gain: knowing Christ," sparked by a meeting with his friend Tom Phillips, then chairman of the Raytheon Company.

"I went to see Tom and he had a peace about himself," Colson explained. "I said to him, 'What has happened?' He said, 'I have accepted Jesus Christ and I'm committing my life to him.' I fumbled around and changed the subject, but those words stuck with me." Phillips then read him the chapter in C. S. Lewis's *Mere Christianity*, in which the author speaks of pride and self-conceit as "spiritual cancer," leaving Colson feeling as if he'd been stabbed in the stomach.

"C. S. Lewis didn't know it, but he was writing that chapter about me," remembered Colson. "I went out to the automobile, but I couldn't drive that car—I was in a flood of tears. I became aware of my sin and called out to God." Colson's collision with God ended up taking him back to jail for good, this time with a new career—as founder of Prison Fellowship Ministries, a Virginia-based organization that spreads the gospel in prisons and seeks reforms of the criminal justice system. I asked Colson if despondent inmates serving life sentences really got a lift from airy tidings such as "Don't worry, God loves you." He gave me an immediate and forceful response.

"Those guys are the easiest to get through to. Because they have never had anybody love them before in their lives."

What I was getting so far was really the same basic message that my college companion Sarah had communicated to me long ago: God was love and love was everything. But who was God? During the course of an afternoon at the Essex House in New York City, I tried many times to get Billy Graham to pinpoint the God he knew—was He a presence, a feeling, a voice? I figured if anyone could show me the direct divine route it would be the Abraham of Born-Again Christianity who, in 1985, at the age of sixty-six, had preached to 104 million people in 60 countries. What did Graham know that no one else knew, The Word that had been sought out by potentates from Winston

Churchill to Pope John Paul II? Before Dwight Eisenhower died, it was Billy Graham he turned to for assurance on his next destination: "He said to me, 'How can I be sure that I'm going to go to heaven?' " remembers Graham.

"But I don't think of myself in any sense as a superstar. I mean, there's nothing different about me," insisted Graham, who grew up milking Guernseys on a second-generation farm in Charlotte, North Carolina. "I'm just handing out messages to people saying 'God loves you, you're important to God, you need to let Christ into your heart in order to have your sins forgiven and in order to get to heaven. And you must repent of your sins and change your way of living.' I am just the messenger. God does the converting.

"You were born the first time physically. You are born the second time when the spirit of God comes into your heart and changes your attitudes and changes your goals in life."

I wanted to know if, after some forty years of preaching, he felt he had accomplished his mission. He shook his head sadly.

"No," he started out in a near whisper. "I had thought in the earlier days of my ministry that I would live to see a great, massive turning to God throughout the world—and the problems that we're now facing in the world would be solved in my lifetime.

"Then all of a sudden came World War II and atomic bombs. And I began to realize that the whole thing was up for grabs and that man was going to live out an uncertain future. The only certainty in the whole world is Christ."

Hmmm, the only certainty there is in the whole world is Christ, how can anybody know this, in no uncertain terms? No human can know this, of this I was certain. Why should I listen to Billy Graham? Who knew what he did off-hours? Although the Jim Bakker sex-and-money scandal was two years away, there had already been plenty of self-righteous Elmer Gantry types who claimed to be at the right hand of God, scarred by sleazy dalliances or gambling away their flocks' donations. Billy Graham seemed squeaky clean, but who could you believe?

The telephone rang in the hotel room, and it was picked up by Larry Ross, Graham's longtime press aide. Ross told us that the UPI photographer was down in the lobby, and that he was going downstairs to meet him. When the door closed, the preacher who had been ruddy and effusive turned white and silent, he actually looked as if he was getting sick. I asked him what was wrong. Graham stared at me with incandescent eyes and told me that what was wrong was that he was alone in a hotel room with a woman who wasn't his wife. "This is the first time I've been alone with a woman who wasn't Ruth for as long as I can remember. I'm not even alone with my secretary in a room or in a car when we travel. That's why you don't hear any stories about me: Can you imagine if you and I walked out of this room and someone saw us? Billy Graham coming out of a hotel room with a woman," he said.

"I try to live every day as though I'm living right in the presence of God. [George] Orwell talked about 'Big Brother' watching in his book *1984*. Well, I know that the Lord is watching me at all times, and I have to live in this room here as I have to live a thousand miles from here, exactly the same as I do in my home. I can't be two people; I have to have the same integrity whatever I'm doing. . . . I never in my whole life touched another woman but my wife. Somebody asked me what I wanted on my tombstone and I said, 'He Walked in His Integrity.' "

After witnessing his genuine unease over having to spend fifteen minutes alone with a female journalist, I am sure he deserves that epitaph. Indeed, more than a decade later, Billy Graham, now ailing from Parkinson's disease and about to pass the mantle of the Billy Graham Evangelistic Association to his son Franklin, can rest on his word for building a revival ministry that has remained untarnished by scandal throughout its forty-

six-year history—this with 525 employees and 1995 revenues of
$88 million.

When the interview with Billy Graham in his room at the
Essex House was nearly over, I asked him what it meant "to
give your life to the Lord," an expression that had always both-
ered me. Graham sent me home with the advice to read his book
Peace with God. I didn't open it until several months later on
the train to and from the seminary Timothy attended, where I
spent a horrible weekend with him fighting about Jesus Christ.
From the very first page of chapter one, Billy Graham was reeling me in:

> *You started on the Great Quest the moment you were*
> *born. It was many years perhaps before you realized it,*
> *before it became apparent that you were constantly*
> *searching—searching for something you never had—*
> *searching for something that was more important than*
> *anything in life . . . At moments you have almost been*
> *able to dismiss the quest completely. But always you*
> *have been caught up in it again—always you have had*
> *to come back to your search. . . .*
>
> *All mankind is traveling with you, for all man-*
> *kind is on the same quest . . . we shall never find com-*
> *pleteness and fullness apart from fellowship with Him.*

I put down the book and gazed at the whir of greenery out the
train window. Hadn't I tried everything else? Buddhism, step
aerobics, a French boyfriend, macrobiotics—and where was I?
Down, down, down—in my work, in my love life, in my heart.
Could the Lord really be the only eternal pick-me-up? I liked
the idea that the person of God inhabited this earth with me,
and was not floating in the heavens, threaded through the

clouds, out of space, out of time, out of reach, like I had always imagined the Almighty to be.

Graham brought it on home: "Don't take anyone else's word for God. Find Him for yourself, and then you too will know by the wonderful, warm tug on your heartstrings that He is there *for sure.*"

Almost over the edge, but not quite there, a book entitled *Let Go and Let God* pushed me over to Billy Graham's side. I had laughed off this paperback with its cover of soft-focus daisies as a nothing of a read when it was given to me by a faith healer months earlier. But when I went back to it in my newfound exultation, it was everything I needed to hear.

"Let go of your problems, let go of your anxieties, and let God fill you with kindness and love," Albert E. Cliffe instructs his readers.

"Let go those things in life which have kept you from happiness, and let God."

Let go. Surrender. Boy was I ready to fall back into a cushion that would hold me up, that would never fail me. Let Go and Let God? Why not? In this humbled, jumbled Lord-have-mercy state, the most incredible thing occurred. God came calling in a ballroom of the Watergate Hotel, scene of the fall of the President's Men.

I was at a trunk show of semiprecious jewelry by the late Brazilian designer Haroldo Burle Marx at a store off the hotel lobby. There were lots of congressional wives and Washington socialites there, chums of the store's owner, Alta Leath, the ex-wife of former Texas congressman Marvin Leath. While I usually liked to work a crowd like this for story material, instead I sat in a corner locked in conversation with Patty Hutchens, an artist and the wife of a Presbyterian minister. I relayed tales of Timothy, and she told me about the years that she and her husband and three children lived in Israel. They had converted to Judaism, and had decided to move to the Jewish state. But once they got there, they were told by the Israeli Orthodox rabbinate that their conversion was not acceptable in Israel unless they renounced their belief in Jesus as Messiah. They could not.

Patty went from a few tears streaming mascara down her cheeks to heaving sobs as she told me her saga A friend later told me that when she saw me with Patty my mouth was open and I was motionless. Because what I was getting was that her God and my God were one and the same. Suddenly Patty said, "Let's move to a quiet room where we can pray."

We walked past the women in Chanel suits mulling over amethysts the size of grapes and found an empty banquet room where the curtains were drawn. Patty then led me through a prayer about my God of Abraham that ended with a plea for the Lord to fill my heart. And presto, in a rush, the way Billy Graham had promised, God was in there. I felt a burst of fire, a warm flood inside, lighter in the head, all over. The taxi ride back to UPI was glorious. The skies were turquoise and filled with sheer brushes of clouds. I had not seen colors or felt nature with such acuity since 1973 in Boulder, when we chopped up peyote buttons and drank them down in a vanilla milkshake before a Joe Cocker–Leon Russell concert. When I heard them do "She Came in Through the Bathroom Window," I had a vision of floating through the sky in a gauzy dress, my long hair trailing me, and curling my body into the bathroom of my childhood in Oak Park, Illinois. It was a beautiful Technicolor vision of magic and light.

So this is where I had landed after a lifetime of looking for a God I could trust, I could touch. As bizarre as it seemed, it really was a predictable next step in a journey that had started as a child reared on Holocaust stories. Thoughts of the Catholic angels who had saved my mother remained seared in my consciousness. I never shook the image of Helene Steinberg going to mass, and taking communion from a priest who knew she was Jewish. Timing is everything and I was ripe for this blast. It was as if God was blowing his winds into me, with a whoosh that wouldn't quit. Spectacular as it was, the bliss was short-lived.

Yet for the weeks I was there I was a maniac about the Lord, carrying on to anyone who would listen—to friends, to strangers at the Safeway. A Maxfield Parrish poster called "Ecstasy" that hung over my bed in college depicts a beatific woman in red-gold light standing on a mountain, her face to the sky. She had total tranquillity, a quality I aspired to but never internalized. When I looked at "Ecstasy" post-Watergate, that was me. It was in this hallelujah-God-frenzy that I started going out with the man I would marry.

Just before Thanksgiving, a friend of mine at UPI, Karl Gude, was hired to be the art director of the Associated Press in New York City. We threw him a going away party at a club called Déjà Vu, where an old friend of Karl's, a stalky architect in an army surplus shirt and a skinny tie and a blue jean jacket, asked me if he could buy me a beer. His name was Chuck and his eyes were see-through blue and I said yeah, sure, Rolling Rock if they have it. He came back to the table holding two icy long-necked bottles and we talked about nothing in particular. The way he looked at me made me feel like a teenager. When I noticed that it was after 6 P.M. I leaped up from the table to call Timothy—we had a standing 6 P.M. phone date each night. I returned and Chuck was talking to Ann, a colleague from UPI. I was happy for Ann, maybe she and Chuck would happen—I was already taken, hopelessly taken.

Sipping the beer, my mood grew dark. Timothy had not been in his dorm room when I telephoned. Chuck would tell me months later that I left without thanking him for the beer or saying good-bye. But I got to see him a couple of days later when he and Ann double-dated with Karl and me at the Lebanese Taverna restaurant in nearby Arlington, Virginia.

It was a cold night and Chuck had on an olive green and red thrift-store sweater that looked about a hundred years old. My impulse was to stroke him, to see if the sweater was as soft as it looked, to see if his arms and chest were as hard as they appeared. This is what I remember about that night: that I talked and Chuck listened, he was a wonderful listener, he listened with his whole body, with his eyes, with long legs that were touching my knees. So guess what I was talking about? Jesus and Bob Dylan. I told him how great it was that the touchstone of our generation had opened up his soul to the spiritual potential in all of life, beyond the dogma of his Judaism, with his *Slow Train Coming* album composed during his awakening to the Lord. Chuck was staring so, so hard. I felt as if I could say anything to this person with The Eyes, that I didn't have to censor any parts of my personality.

I was used to being careful not to appear too smart or too eccentric when trying to impress a new man. But Chuck was right there with me, I could tell he wasn't judging, he was just taking it all in—and I was very weird that evening. The restaurant was cold and he took off his sweater and gave it to me. When I put it on it was as if the musky smelling sheath of Chuck now covered me, captured me. I was in his skin, and it was right, like I had always been there, a déjà vu of sorts, the name of the bar where we met. Years later, when I read him the installment in my diary about our dinner at Lebanese Taverna, I asked him what he was thinking during my ramblings on religion. He told me he was thinking that he wanted to sleep with me.

But we didn't for a long time—I wanted the Slow Train with this one after the Orient Express that came screeching to a halt with everyone else. Our first dates were spent eating mussels and making out in a dark booth at the Childe Harold, then going back to his apartment to listen to Dylan's *Shot of Love* and make out some more. I liked this Chuck with the craggy face and remarkable attention span; he was something that other men had failed to be—he was There.

So that I wouldn't get too carried away with this man-of-the-moment who was now tweaking my fantasies of going to Bendel's bridal section and booking the Standard Club ballroom in Chicago, I read all my journals, starting with junior year at Oak Park High School. What I realized when surveying these books was that I had been fantasizing about Mr. Wrongs all my dating life. This Chuck was not impossible. Chuck was possible. Hmmm. But this notion of a possible man, not an impossible man who I'd have to toil for and suffer to win, was a bit unnerving. Wasn't winning the whole game? Then moving on? It seemed to be with most women I knew.

We were hooked on tense love, on dangerous love. When stability and commitment came our way, we bolted. Yet this guy had real potential. He was strong and silent and played the guitar like C.T. of California, was a Renaissance man like Timothy of Texas. And—he was All-American, springing from an English family that settled before the Revolution on the Eastern Shore of Maryland. He was, as my friends said, my type.

But Chuck took my type into a broadened dimension, because although he was slow and easy and artistic and tall, he also seemed interested in being the architect who would build my dreams. I cut five inches off my hair, and spent $250 at Loehmann's. Chuck was by my side, dependable and predictable, eating Chinese food from the containers and working it off on walks along the Potomac River. Things were normal for a change, not wrenching and wild.

The blinding God phase was waning, edged out by something else—very solid and very real. This Chuck who drove a battered blue 1972 Porsche convertible was bringing me closer to what I really wanted, had always wanted, and it wasn't to sit alone on my couch reading the Bible—it was marriage and kids. For this gift of a good man, I was feeling expectant and blessed. Then the storm came.

The afternoon of January 19, 1986, I was in the midst of writing a long profile on sculptor Louise Nevelson, who was 86 at the time, feisty as a 40-year-old, still maneuvering heavy tools and producing enormous bronzes. Energized by the tape of her voice playing back into my headset, my sentences were flowing and ripe. This mood burst with the phone call every son and daughter knows will come one day: "Daddy had a heart attack." It was my sister Fran's terrified voice from Hawaii, where she was vacationing, to my desk at the UPI bureau in Washington. "Come to San Diego. It's bad . . . but it could be worse. He's alive."

I slumped over at my desk. Two hours later, I was headed to San Diego where my parents were spending the winter. Chuck had picked me up at UPI, helped me pack, driven me to National Airport, walked me onto the plane, told the stewardess on the United flight to take care of me, kissed me, and told me he loved me. I told him to water my plants, take care of my cat, Max, and pray.

When I got to my parents' condominium in Coronado after midnight, I climbed into my father's empty side of the bed next to my mother, his wife of thirty-four years. His old, navy plaid bathrobe hung on the door. Although I was scared, I was certain he'd be back in that bathrobe he'd worn my whole life. Nothing could happen to Ted Krasnow, who was so sharp, so funny, so indomitable.

The next week the shuttle *Challenger* exploded, a globe-shaking horror that coincided with the beginning of the most wretched journey of my family's lives, a pain so vast and unrelenting it felt as if it would swallow us. Not only did Ted Krasnow not get better, but with each day that passed and each new drug that he took and each new specialist who poked him he got worse. It took him five weeks of slipping in and out of a coma to die, and it was an ugly death triggered by the treatment, not the disease. The heparin and streptokinase he was given, called thrombolytic therapy, to "thin the blood and prevent clotting," as his doctors said, led to bleeding in his brain and total deterioration of his body.

He went into the hospital a brilliant and vibrant man who presided over a large furniture company he had built over the course of forty years. When he died six weeks later he couldn't talk, walk, or eat. My distraction from the torturous pain was to busy myself keeping copious notes in my journal, as if I were covering a tragedy that was not my own.

When I walked into his small room at an ill-equipped Coronado hospital my father said, "Iris, let me see you." He was hooked up to an oxygen pump, a catheter, and an intravenous tube leading to several dangling bottles. I stood at the side of his bed and we talked about journalism and the beauty of Coronado. He was as coherent as ever, but his voice was raspy and weak. During the five minutes I spent with him he was clutching his head with both hands. He asked me to call the nurse and tell her he was getting a headache. The nurse came in and gave him some Tylenol, then he grabbed my arm and said, "This is my daughter. She's a UPI reporter in Washington, D.C." I can still hear that voice, thick with pride.

Within an hour he fell into a coma as his head filled with blood. He was moved to a larger hospital in San Diego. Over the course of a six-week stupor there were three incidents during which he showed clarity. One Saturday he started writing simple sentences such as "Where am I?" and "Where's the family?" Two weeks later he said my name while I was leaning over him. The following week he was downright chatty, saying things like "son of a bitch" and "I don't want you kids to worry." He beamed when we told him his Chicago Bears had won the Super

Bowl, and started asking about his office. We were sure that we had all finally turned the corner, especially after his neurosurgeon assured us that he'd be released in three weeks and that within three months "You will never remember me or this hospital."

On Valentine's Day, my father quit talking, and his eyes became fixed at half-mast. A CAT scan showed the fluid had built up again in the brain, and a shunt, or a clear plastic drainage tube, was put in to alleviate the swelling. That procedure appeared to be doing the job. The next day he started speaking French, telling jokes in a Yiddish accent, swearing at the nurse, and smiling when he saw my sister's baby girl, Marissa. For the first time, he ate by himself, a popsicle, and he asked for spaghetti, bagels, and a "drink as big as a house." We were on a grand high when the neurosurgeon gave us this jolly prediction: "Ted will be on the golf course in three weeks."

Days later, my father's heart stopped. The death of Theodore Jacob Krasnow at the age of sixty-seven shattered everything; it was a black hole of agony, the death of all joy, the death of my faith. While he fought for his life those grisly weeks, I never stopped crying out to God and anyone else who could help. But no one came, only silence and destruction to the pillar of our lives. Someone sent our family a copy of Rabbi Harold Kushner's *When Bad Things Happen to Good People*, and I threw it in the garbage. So much for the grace of God. Of this I was now convinced: Bad things happen because people are running the universe, not a good God, people like the doctor who gave my father a then experimental drug that turned out to be more dangerous than his illness.

Since we were lulled into thinking my father's health was improving, our focus wasn't on mapping out alternative courses of action. Only in hindsight did we realize we should have been more forceful about changing his therapies and calling in new doctors. Although my sister is an ace litigator at a large Chicago law firm, we never sued. The Krasnows had no strength to play back the blackest days of our lives. What could we get in return? Not the tall man with the big voice who would tell me when I was down, "Now, Iris, go look in the mirror, and shout 'I'm great, I'm great, I'm great.'"

My father was gone, and what remained? Two siblings and a mother I loved deeply. A new boyfriend who not only nourished my plants and made Max the cat very happy but also bought blue flannel sheets with sheep skipping across them and put them on my bed for my homecoming. A glamorous job. A Christmas card with a family picture from the Husseins of Jordan. But the tears still came in torrents throughout the day—the only respite was in sleep, which came in agitated spurts. My father was in every dream, sitting at our Formica kitchen table in Oak Park wearing his old blue plaid bathrobe. He was the person who had been the biggest influence on me; I had gauged my life in terms of his evaluations, my victories had been fuller because of the glory I saw reflected in his eyes.

My brother, Greg, who lives in Tucson, and who has the same business knack as my father, literally shut down.

"I lost five years of my life," Greg told me. "From the day it happened, I just stopped. I felt like it was over, you know, like there was no need to do anything else. I went through everything—drinking, odd jobs, I basically couldn't function. It was more than losing a best friend, it was like losing your life but being alive to feel the agony."

Today, Greg is approaching his fortieth birthday and works as a real estate agent in Tucson, where he lives with his wife, Nancy. He says that even now, nearly a decade later, he feels as if there is something he wants to tell our father every day. After losing Theodore Krasnow, my life, too, became, for the first time, fully mine to figure out, to celebrate, to live. This realization was terrifying.

In those first raw months, driving to the UPI office listening to a cassette playing "Lean on Me," I'd have to pull over to the side of the road because of sobs that shook my entire body. I'd break down at the sight of an empty chair, or a plate of spaghetti and meatballs, which he loved, or older men walking in downtown Washington in their trench coats carrying briefcases. My father's London Fog trench coat hung in his closet, never to be worn again. His briefcase—that briefcase, it took the longest time for any of us to go near that damn thing, crammed with papers scrawled with his fresh handwriting. Throughout it all, Chuck was by my side, rocking me in his arms as I cried and cried and cried. He loved me, but I could not love him back. How could I give love, that abundance of soulful energy? You cannot give love when your heart is cracking.

I dragged myself into UPI and tried to get excited about hot personalities and breaking trends. But the only person I had any interest in interviewing was my father, a man who was smarter and funnier than any of the celebrities I had profiled, but who had never even spoken into his own daughter's tape recorder.

Throughout my life, when things got rough my dad would tell me, "You gotta swing with it, Iris." Swing with life's thrashes and you'll always, inevitably, land on your feet. Even in his death, he didn't let me down. Because I did swing with it, with every long day, through the phone calls with my mother as she sat on her beige tweed couch in Chicago next to my father's empty recliner chair. I swung with it in the mornings when the sun would stream through my windows and make me angry that the world was going on just like it did before. I swung with it during the nights of fright when I couldn't shake the vision of my father flying alone in his simple pine coffin in the belly of a United flight while his bereaved family sat huddled together above him in the passenger cabin.

I swung and I swung, and I think I went forward, although

I couldn't tell at the time. But there had to be movement, because I still showed up for work and I ate my Lean Cuisine, and I did some of the best journalism of my career. These are the stories that helped me heal—interviews with Elisabeth Kübler-Ross and Elie Wiesel and a piece on a mountain climbing course for disabled adults in the High Sierras.

Although this assortment is diverse, there is an underlying theme: These people were swinging through obstacles far greater than mine or anyone else I knew. Hearing their stories actually ended up rerouting my life, a life that had forever been led In Search Of more and better, be it a more brilliant career, a tighter body, or happiness that was lasting and real. Through their insights I got closer to my true nature, away from the relentless climb, into the sacred flow of the moment and toward that elusive force called God.

I gravitated toward Kübler-Ross for obvious reasons: she was, quite simply, the guru of death. In addition to being the author of the landmark book *On Death and Dying*, which first outlined the five stages of coping with the loss of loved ones, from denial to acceptance, Kübler-Ross was also an unquestioning believer in life after death. As I drove the three hours from Washington, D.C., to her farm in Headwaters, Virginia, I wondered if this woman who had been coaching the terminally ill for some twenty years could put me back in touch with Theodore Krasnow.

I arrived at a 250-acre paradise in the Shenandoah hills where pines pierced the sky and peacocks and burros roamed free. The Swiss-born Kübler-Ross, a five-foot firecracker in jeans, a white sweatshirt, and hiking boots, was exuberant from having just assisted in the birth of twin baby lambs.

Rather than settle into her slow golden years, Kübler-Ross, then sixty-two, had taken on the toughest assignment of her career. Her new book, *AIDS: The Ultimate Challenge*, had led her to form Death, Dying and Transition workshops for AIDS patients and toward plans to start a hospice for AIDS babies on her property. But here in ultraconservative Highland County, Virginia, there were residents who were so appalled that Kübler-Ross wanted to bring AIDS to their neighborhood that she had received several threats that her farm would be burned down. (Several years later, Healing Waters was destroyed in a fire; arson was suspected.)

I asked her if the threats made her fear for her life.

Kübler-Ross was curled up in an oversized corduroy chair, knitting a pale blue scarf flecked with lavender. Her callused fingers moved swiftly and she didn't look up as she responded in a voice made hoarse from years of cigarettes.

"No, I feel totally protected," she said, laughing softly. "And if I have to make the transition, I'm certainly not afraid of it."

She explained how spending two decades at the side of the terminally ill, a career that restored dignity to the dying process and helped pioneer the hospice movement, had evolved into a passionate certainty about afterlife. This belief was bolstered by her documentation of some twenty thousand out-of-body experiences reported by people who said they were aware of shedding their physical selves "like a butterfly" when they were near death. Kübler-Ross further described the transition from life to more life, and the skepticism she was fielding from doctors and scientists.

"Those who are not yet ready to hear about it will be pleasantly surprised," she said, drawing deeply on a smoke. "How do I verify that those who die are really alive? That's easy to do when you look at dying children. For example, on a July Fourth weekend, three members of a family are in an accident and the children are sent to burn units and intensive care units. I sit with the youngest child . . . and shortly before she dies, there is a change that takes place that I can pick up very fast. It's like she has no more anxiety, a peace comes over her. Then I touch her and say, 'Are you going to share with me what you experience?'

"And she looks at me like she's looking through me and says, 'Everything is okay now. My brother Peter is already waiting for me.' But Peter was sent to another hospital's burn unit. And when I leave the ICU, I have a message that the burn unit called and Peter died ten minutes ago. And the only mistake I made is to say, 'Yes, I know.' They think you're cuckoo. But I have never had a dying child who didn't mention somebody who preceded them in death."

She chuckled and added: "It just helps to know there is no end to your work."

Tossing her knitting aside and springing from her chair, Kübler-Ross picked up an orange velour caterpillar from a basket on the floor. "This is what I show to dying children. I tell them 'Your body is just a caterpillar. When you die, the caterpillar will release the butterfly.' Ross reached into a slit in the caterpillar and pulled out a tiny monarch butterfly.

"And I tell them, 'The butterfly is the immortal part of the human being that flies up. The only thing that is mortal, the body, goes back to the soil.'" She sat back down in her chair and stared intensely: "You don't think this life is all there really is, do you?"

On the long drive home through the hushed Virginia hills at sunset, I remembered hugging my father's lifeless body, wrapped in a sterile hospital gown. As I lay my head on his cold, hard chest, this thought came up for me sharply and instantly: He is not in here. Reflecting on this after meeting Elisabeth Kübler-Ross, I was overcome with a knowing that even as my father's body was lowered into the icy ground of Chicago in late February, he had already escaped, that his spirit was freed, living in me, in my sister, in my brother, in my mother, in his brother, in his sister, in the hundreds of people he had touched. Because of Kübler-Ross's toy caterpillar with a butterfly inside its tummy, I felt happier than I had felt in months.

But losing a parent is an insidious thing, it's two steps forward and five steps back. Some days I would start to get better only to wake up the next morning feeling like someone had ripped my heart out of my chest. My relationship with God fluctuated between the cordial and the incensed. Yet confronting my demons about religion was tough to avoid. In the months immediately after my father's death, God continued to dominate the news as busted materialists went scavenging around for spiritual salvation. In March 1986, the Saturday Evening Post featured a lead story on Billy Graham, "The World Is His Pulpit." In April 1986, the cover story of the New Age Journal was on "Spiritual Hunger in America: A Generation's Unlikely Leap of Faith." In December 1986, a cover story of The Washingtonian magazine trumpeted that "God Is Back." And that same month a rendering of Jesus was on the cover of The Atlantic, teasing this article inside: "Who Do Men Say That I Am?" I read these stories with a brittle heart, convinced that God had forsaken me—or worse, had never really been there at all. This thought had occupied my mind before when I first read Night, Holocaust survivor Elie Wiesel's autobiographical book in which he wonders if God died in Hitler's death camps.

"Never shall I forget the faces of the children, whose bodies I saw turned into wreaths of smoke beneath a silent blue sky," Wiesel writes. "Never shall I forget those flames which consumed my faith forever. Never shall I forget those moments which murdered my God and my soul and turned my dreams to dust." Wiesel is reminded of the nightmare every day: a blue "A-7713" is etched into his arm.

I tried to say my old prayers at night, but they came out feebly, falsely, as if I were spewing someone else's lines. Thank you, God—for what? I had Let Go and Let God, and see what happened? Darkness and death. And not just for me. In the midst of my own despair the United States bombed Libya and the nuclear power plant at Chernobyl exploded. It was during one of my blackest stages that I had the chance to interview Elie Wiesel when he was visiting Washington to receive a B'nai B'rith award at the Adas Israel Congregation. The author, known as the voice of the Holocaust, let me accompany him in the limousine during the forty-five-minute ride to Dulles airport, then agreed to a subsequent session that took place at his apartment in New York City. The interest in Wiesel was twofold: to get lost in a subject greater than my own suffering, and to explore how he now felt about a God he had described many years earlier as being "murdered" in Auschwitz. This notion of a dead God intrigued me; in fact, the idea made perfect sense: God was dead and that's why life was lousy.

When I met Wiesel and he began to speak to me, I could not take my eyes off his face, a face of features that prodded the conscience. Pale and pointed, with haunted eyes, his face was a canvas of mortality.

I asked Elie Wiesel who God was to him long ago in the camps, and how that compared to his God of now.

"I'm still wondering, I don't know. I'm asking the question and there is no answer to the question. Where was humanity? And also where was God? I still wonder what was His role? Just as you cannot conceive Auschwitz without God, you cannot conceive it with God. And that's a trap, so what is the answer?"

In 1944, Wiesel was herded into a cattle car along with his family in the Hungarian town of Sighet. When they arrived at Auschwitz, men were ordered to the left and women to the right. As Wiesel walked to the left, his father clutching his arm, he lost sight of his mother and younger sister forever. Wiesel also wrote of babies being tossed into ditches of fire. When a group of Jews began to recite Kaddish, the prayer for the dead, Wiesel felt fury with God. As he exclaimed in *Night*: "Why should I bless His name? What had I to thank Him for?"

His father, Shlomo, died several months later in Buchenwald, the labor camp from which Wiesel was liberated. He was moved to France in 1945 along with other orphaned Jewish children, and found out that his two older sisters, Hilda and Batya, had also survived. Yet this God whom he had doubted in a fury had also obviously blessed him, by saving two siblings and by giving him a wife, Marion, who was a concentration camp survivor as well. They would have a son together, Shlomo-Elisha, and Wiesel would go on to win the Nobel Prize for Peace in 1986. When I interviewed Wiesel, his son was a fourteen-year-old who loved baseball and computers and rock music, "the center of my life," as Wiesel called him. When Elie Wiesel was fourteen, he had just been moved to Auschwitz.

Starting with Jacob, wrestling with God has always been the way of the Jewish religion. I often wished for the assuredness that many Christians I knew experienced. But even when the love of God eluded me, the consistency of the rituals of Judaism never ceased to console. The predictability of the seasons and celebrations in the Jewish calendar provided a rhythm to my life that no one could ever take away. When I asked Elie Wiesel where he had evolved in his relationship with God, he responded this way:

"I'm a religious person; always have been," he said. "I never stopped studying the Bible, Talmud, Hassidism. At the same time, the problems remain open. I will continue to question until the end of my life."

While attempting to make my peace with both God and death, a friend told me I had to find the book *You Gotta Keep Dancing* by Tim Hansel. One Saturday at the Washington Hilton pool I read, from cover to cover, the saga of the author who almost died in a mountain climbing accident. Six weeks later I was backpacking with a disabled group of campers and Hansel in a course he created called Go for It. Many were on crutches or confined to wheelchairs, but under Hansel's instruction they were learning to rock climb at eight thousand feet in the High Sierras.

Hansel had started the rigorous Go for It program for physically challenged adults, a rigorous five days of climbing, hiking, fasting, and praying, after surviving a fall that nearly killed him. On an ice climb in August 1974, his crampons became encrusted with snow and his self-arrest with an ax failed at thirteen thousand feet on Palisades Glacier near Yosemite. He flipped over a cornice and landed on the back of his neck five stories below on solid ice, crushing vertebrae, collapsing spinal discs, and shooting fragments of bone into his neck. Miraculously, he survived with nearly full movement of his arms and legs. But he will never escape the chronic pain that will saddle him for a lifetime.

You Gotta Keep Dancing is an account of what he describes as the "peace I have discovered inside the pain." While sitting on a rock ledge covered with gnarled manzanita, the wind and the sun and majesty of sky jolting every sense, Hansel explained how being miserable is a choice, and that however badly he hurt, "I choose joy."

As we spoke, camper Sally Krohn inched her way toward us propped up on metal crutches, dragging one leg encased in a full brace. Crippled from childhood by polio, Krohn, nineteen, was sweating and crying but not stopping. Watching Krohn, I was determined to push my own body like I had never done before. So, after eighteen-year-old Julie Kelly, confined to a wheelchair from spina bifida, rappeled down the mountain secured by five sets of rope, I, too, jumped backward off the steep cliff, into exhilaration, and into acceptance.

"You were made for this," Tim Hansel bellowed to me the second I landed all in one piece. After Summit Expedition, I was

ready to start kicking open new doors again, and to leave my
heartache in the High Sierras. When I got down from our camp-
site, I was overcome with an urge to live with a vengeance, I
couldn't wait to start peeling away the layers that had slowed
me down, to burrow as deep as I could go, to the wellspring, to
the source. I was made for this, indeed. To leap off mountains
and charge ahead, not stop and stew about what had been lost.
Great passion can be released by pain.

YOUR TROUBLE BEGINS WHEN YOU GET WHAT YOU WANT

Soon after watching valiant kids force their bodies to peak performance by tapping into their spiritual reservoirs I said yes to
a proposal of marriage from Chuck, who grew up in the farming
town of Centreville, Maryland, population two thousand, due
east of the Chesapeake Bay. Chuck was a man who could show
me a few things about the marrow of existence that I had sa-
vored in the High Sierra, and that Henry David Thoreau had
relished at Walden Pond.

Chuck was the best of every boyfriend I ever had. He was
rugged and his eyes were kind, and I knew I wanted his children.
He proposed in a cabin set in a lush valley between Cacapon
Mountain and Warm Springs Ridge in Berkeley Springs, West
Virginia.

I announced our engagement this way in my diary:

"Charles E. Anthony asked me to marry him on a chilly
morning in a double bed in a log cabin. I can't believe it. The
path is finally cleared to move on and have a real life with real
plans. I feel like Chuck and I are a balanced couple: I, up, down
and all around; He, steady and methodical. Our children will
have curls."

Onward, as my father used to say, onward to the rest of
my life, which I was ready, oh, so ready, to begin. This urgency

to domesticate was expedited by the flawed, but scary, new demographic study that appeared in all the major media. Co-authored by Yale sociologist Neil Bennett, the study concluded that white, college-educated women who are still single at thirty only have a twenty percent chance of marrying. By the age of thirty-five, the odds supposedly drop to 5 percent, and women still single at forty "are more likely to be killed by a terrorist" than make it down the aisle with a groom, reported an article in the June 2, 1986, *Newsweek*.

We found a hip, Reform rabbi transplanted from Portland, Oregon, to Chicago who said he would marry us if Chuck vowed to raise Jewish children and explore Judaism himself. Chuck had been raised as a Methodist, but when he was in high school his father, a conservative Korean War hero, had quit the church in protest when the Methodists provided sanctuary to Vietnam conscientious objectors. So there were no deep religious ties to sever, and raising children in the unity of one faith was important to both of us. Under a chuppa at the Standard Club of Chicago we said yes on Saturday night, March 12, 1988, and I became a Wife, dressed in a white silk shantung dress, carrying red roses and white lilies. A light snow fell outside.

During our honeymoon in a villa wedged into a cliff on St. Barts in the French West Indies, we drank Heinekens and talked about having four children by the time we were forty, which for me was seven years away. We went right to work. Five weeks later I was pregnant. Three months later during a sonogram no heartbeat could be found. By that following March I had conceived again during a return trip to St. Barts to celebrate our first anniversary. As the pregnancy progressed I was transported to a blathering state, hormonal and happy and hopeful. For the first time in several baby-craving years, I could look at a woman with a bulge in her belly and not feel inadequate. Remember that stage when you wanted a child more than anything else and what you had instead was a chain of childish boyfriends? Thank God for the Chucks of the world, the guys who finally came through for us. Each night, I'd prop pillows around my throbbing back and abdomen and scribble love letters to our unborn son. Here's the last one, issued a month before his arrival:

> *Dear Baby Boy:*
>
> *I've loved holding you in my womb, being ripe with life during the past nine months. You have filled me with pure energy every long week of the way. At first I worried that you weren't moving enough, hard enough, often enough. But then we saw the sonogram and your tiny fingers stroking your cheek. And now, at 38 weeks, I feel you all the time, your feet and shoulders, the smooth curve of your rump, your head pressing on my bladder.*
>
> *We are all ready for you, our beloved, long-awaited child. You've got a sturdy oak crib with candy-striped flannel sheets, new blue curtains in your room, fresh paint—everything new for your new life, our new life. It's so amazing to think you are ours from the first second you come out. By carrying you, the hole deep inside of me that has always been so impossible to fill is brimming with anticipation of holding you, loving you.*
>
> *Will you turn to me, the voice you have heard the most, as soon as you are born? What goes on deep in that womb, where you swim in my liquid and love? Come out peacefully.*
>
> *Your Mother*

On December 22, 1989, after a fast labor on one of the coldest nights in Washington history, Theodore Jacob Anthony was born, weighing seven and a half pounds. When I saw this baby with my eyes and Chuck's long body it was a melding of soul and heart, a completion of self. Everything came together, a

culmination of waiting and dreaming and scheming and praying. We anointed him with his grandfather's name: Theodore
translates in Greek to "Lover of God." Our son came home from
Columbia Hospital for Women in Washington, D.C., on Christmas Day in a red flannel stocking. As a birth present Chuck gave
me a one-hundred-year-old silver locket engraved with floral
sprigs that opened up to encase a picture of our baby.

God, is this heaven? I was now everything I had ever
wanted to be—Mother and Wife, Wife and Mother. I couldn't
believe it! I had done it; I had achieved the Crowning Achievement for women who worked too much, loved too much, lived
too much, had too much—I had married and given birth. Voilà!
So there! No more sun-dried tomato and chevre salads eaten at
the restaurant of the month with the man of the month. Mother
and Wife, that was me! Permanence, at last! The elation broke
as soon as we left the hospital.

That Christmas night we brought Theo home he cried from
midnight to 5:30 A.M. Blurry-eyed and beat, I called the nurse
at the hospital who had coached me through breastfeeding and
who had jotted her direct line down and said "Call any time,
night or day." I told her I had tried everything—walked with
him, fed him, burped him, sung him Camp Agawak songs,
rocked and rocked and rocked him. What was wrong? She asked
me if he had on a clean diaper. Hmmm, a clean diaper? I
checked his Huggie Ultratrim and sure enough, it was caked
with old, dried poop. She laughed, and I cried, great, weary,
heaving sobs.

Mother and Wife? Your trouble begins when you get what
you want. When I was skinny and single I wanted to be pregnant
and married. Now I was everything I had ever wanted to be, but
who had I become? Lying in our king-size bed, tiny Theo asleep
next to me, I felt like a blob. My stomach, stretched taut for
nine months, was now blobby and soft. My mind, acute with
expectation for nine months, was now blobby and obtuse. My

heart, surging with joy for nine months, was now blobby and blue. Oh, God, what had I done? I started having racy dreams about my preblob life. About Jean the Frenchman I had met at age twenty-six on a Club Med vacation in Morocco, and the two weeks spent with him at the lip of the Indian Ocean in a black-lace string bikini. About my chat with King Hussein at his palace. About drawing on paper tablecloths with crayons and flirting with Manhattan men at the Un Deux Trois Cafe. About being nineteen in the summer of 1975 in a halter top made out of a giant silk scarf.

Where was the mystical energy I had soared on through pregnancy, that sensual At-One-Ment-with-Child? I loved having a cleavage. I loved my undulating belly, the outline of a foot attached to a mystery person growing inside. I loved gaining forty-two pounds. I loved life, it permeated every cell. And now? Who was I? I remember the day that Chuck, all slickered up in a flannel shirt and bolo tie and khakis, went back to work full-time after a week spent at home with a petulant wife and wailing newborn. He was grinning and waving as he climbed into his red Nissan truck. I was standing there in my gray bathrobe, Theo sleeping under my neck. So, this was it, the place I had been yearning, burning, to reach. It was January 1990, a new year, a new decade, I had a husband and child—I had arrived. Why did I feel so melancholy?

I spent most of the baby's first six weeks in that gray bathrobe my mother bought me at Lord & Taylor sometime during the late eighteenth century, trying to recapture the bliss I had felt premotherhood. The woman who wrote that gusher of a love letter to Theo before he was born felt like an alien to this spent woman with tears streaming down her face. Not that I wasn't totally in love with our baby from the start, I was, I couldn't stop kissing him, everywhere, all the time. But something else was going on far more profound than postpartum blues. I was reeling from a fall that came not just after nine months of pregnancy but after nearly two decades of hard living and independence. The me that used to fly solo in and out of men's lives and exotic countries was now Two People, Theo and Iris, a duo that felt as if I were actually carrying fifty people, a hundred people, a packed stadium at a Grateful Dead concert. He was at my breast, in my arms, breathing hotly at my neck every second of the day. I was Theo, he was me, we were fused. Chuck was The Other, the dashing guy in the clean clothes who came home smiling for dinner after a Day in the World to a wife in a gray bathrobe spotted with human excrement and some from Max the cat.

You Go Do What's Really Important

What had we done? Was this the next step for the hot Cosmo Girl who had grown up—to become a tepid frump? Take my post-partum cleavage please, and give me a year alone on a Caribbean beach, flat and svelte and naughty. There was no more daily journalism to plug into for rips of adrenaline; I had left UPI to become a mother at home, with plans to expand my freelance writing business. Hot oil massages for me and Theo from an Ayurvedic practitioner, a baby gift from a friend, helped unjangle muscles and nerves. But when she folded up her table, told me to start Transcendental Meditation again, and walked out the door, I found myself immediately aroused by anxiety, thinking what I had been thinking most of my life, "So, now what?"—this with beautiful Theo asleep on my chest.

Can you believe it? If you've been there, you can. You can believe that when you've spent your whole life wanting what you didn't have, and then you get everything you've ever wanted, all at once your system goes into shock. I mean, who knows how to halt and be where you are when you're used to darting toward some ideal in your imagination that drives you crazy because it doesn't exist?

Perhaps rereading the guides that enraptured me during pregnancy would send me back into the Virgin Moments of New Motherhood. I turned to *A Child Is Born*, Lennart Nilsson's book of month-by-month photographs of life before birth. There is one picture that had never failed to captivate me, a twenty-one-week-old translucent fetus, hands up, legs up, floating within the amniotic sac. You can see every facial feature, every appendage, every vein. That picture used to make me cry: I had a baby like this in me, it was Really real. That picture made me cry again as my newborn with ten perfect fingers and toes was sucking the life out of me; what was Really real felt like someone else's life, some woman off the pages of *Parenting* magazine.

Maybe *What to Expect When You're Expecting* was what I needed. During my pregnancy I had put myself to sleep night after night with that paperback's advice. What did its trio of authors—Arlene Eisenberg, Heidi Eisenberg Murkoff, and Sandee Eisenberg Hathaway—have to say about Great Expectations Gone Awry? This from their segment on Depression:

"Why should roughly one half of all new mothers be so miserable during one of the happiest times of their lives? . . . Hormones, so often the culprit fingered in the case of a woman's mood swings, may offer some rationale. Levels of estrogen and progesterone drop precipitously after childbirth and may trigger depression. . . . But there are a host of other factors that probably contribute to the postpartum blues."

I went down the list of these factors, moving distractedly through "Exhaustion" and "A Feeling of Anticlimax," stopping on "A Sense of Mourning for the Old You," a passage that warns, "Your carefree, possibly career-oriented self, has died (at least temporarily) with your baby's birth." That was it. The Carefree Career Gal I had loathed while I was her seemed like a romantic figure of freedom compared to the shackled me of now. Finally I was everything I ever wanted to be. So why couldn't I, The Woman Who Has It All, muster up the motivation to get off the couch and out of my gray bathrobe? Where was the ignited journalist who catapulted out of bed, put on something skimpy from the Georgetown Cotton Company, and drove the fifteen minutes to UPI singing loudly along with Carly Simon on my tape player to my man of the week: "You're with me now and as long as you stay, Lovin' you's the right thing to do, Lovin' you's the right thing."

It wasn't so much that I hated the new me; it was more like I couldn't figure out who she was. I mean—only a few short months ago I was wearing panty hose and reading *Newsweek*. There's no way to poll the millions of women who have put *What to Expect When You're Expecting* on a never-ending bestseller list, but I would bet real money that most of those readers aren't that different from me—older, know-it-all, had-too-much moms who were quite surprised that what we got after expecting wasn't like anything we ever expected in our life. I don't know about you, but when our firstborn made his debut I was too discombobulated to even bother buying *What to Expect Your Baby's First Year* by the same authors. I knew what to expect—a steamrolled self.

Instead, my primary literary outlet was a myriad of children's catalogs like The Right Start and One Step Ahead that started appearing in the mailbox the second we became parents. And I started shopping and shopping and shopping by phone. Knowing that each new day could bring a new package my way with accoutrements for our prince was the kick I needed. By the beginning of February I changed out of the gray robe into a blue-jean dress and kidproof Eddie Bauer cotton tights so I'd be presentable for the UPS delivery man, a cute, young student.

So here's the kind of gadgets that older moms like me of the Excel-Excel Generation were scarfing up for our long-awaited babes: walkers with flying Mickey Mouse trapeze artists to sharpen hand-eye coordination; black-and-white mobiles for visual stimulation; electric warmers for baby-bottom wipes; bath seats shaped like boats that come with marinas to dock in; video nursery monitors that hook up to TV sets; and European strollers that cost as much as used MGs. Manufacturers were on a lucrative roll with our thing-oriented, Sharper Image generation that had spawned talking bathroom scales and fifteen flavors of vinegar.

Janet Fullwood, a friend from the *Dallas Times Herald* who had transferred to the *Sacramento Bee*, had her first child at the age of thirty-seven, just after Theo was born. We laughed about the extravagant products for yuppie babies, and she told me I wouldn't believe the one she found for her Will: a $1,200 electronic bassinet called Nature's Cradle. Fullwood was selected by the manufacturer, Infant Advantage, to test-market this white, rectangular box with a computerized chip that caused it to rock intermittently. A speaker under the mattress played whooshing wave noises. This space-age cradle that reproduced the sounds and loll of the womb was supposed to make babies more settled and better sleepers, which Fullwood swore they did for her Jetson boy, Will.

Yet my own high-tech deliveries brought by the adorable UPS emissary soon, very soon, got old, very old. Chuck would come home after a day of designing buildings and what had I done? Opened up packages and dangled them in front of a baby who would have been just as delighted to be gnawing on an empty cereal box. I became very mad at Chuck, cussing at the drop of an orthodontically correct pacifier. He told me I needed to get out of the house—alone, without Theo in his Flap Happy sunbonnet, without his McLaren navy plaid umbrella stroller.

Thank God for Bernice, a forty-eight-year-old mother of three from North Carolina who quit high school to raise ten younger brothers and sisters after her mother died in childbirth. My puny burden was nothing for this woman. Thank God for Bernice, the find of my life, who unfrazzled me and made a return to journalism possible. She, along with seventy-one other applicants, came to us from a *Washington Post* ad that asked for "Babysitter/Housekeeper, 2–3 days a week in caring Northwest Washington home with infant." Bernice arrived for her interview forty-five minutes early carrying a black patent leather purse and wearing black patent leather shoes. Her smile was wide and welcoming and wonderful. I asked her if she liked babies.

"I looooove babies," Bernice replied.

Do you like to cook?

"I looooove to cook."

Do you mind doing some ironing?

"I looooove to iron."

Do you have any faults?

"I never stop moving. Makes some folks nervous. And I can't work Sundays. I'm in the church choir."

Bernice started the next day. When Theo was eight weeks old and growing more cantankerous, I sank into a funk because I couldn't seem to please him. Bernice said to me, "Child, get out of the house, we'll be okay, me and Theo."

I said, "But, Bernice, I need to breastfeed him every two hours."

She said, "You've been breastfeeding and breastfeeding, but that boy is hungry."

I said, "But, Bernice, his immune system needs my milk."

She said, "Child, his stomach needs something else."

And so I caved in to this women who had raised three children and ten siblings and read the New Testament for advice. Chuck drove to the Safeway and purchased foul-smelling, foul-tasting chemical milk that turned our fussy Theo into a docile, groggy baby. This Theo who used to wake up shrieking every two hours started to sleep for five-hour stretches. The breastfeeding was cut back to three times a day and we instructed Bernice to fill 'em up on Similac whenever he wanted it in between. Ah, freedom! When the former managing editor of UPI, Barry Sussman, called and asked me to write a piece on power lunches for a new newspaper he was helping to start up, the *Washington Reporter*, I felt that familiar pound in the chest, that surge of adrenaline, as I gave a quick "Yes!"

I pulled on sheer black L'Eggs and a black suit with satin lapels from the Gap and drove to Duke Zeibert's, the mecca for high-voltage Washington lunches. Tossing back Duke's trademark chocolate mints in neon candy shells and watching the capital's power elite line up for their power chicken-in-the-pots, I was the old me, a me that was thrilled to be off the living room couch. That week my research continued as I worked the restaurants in pantyhose all around town. Baby at night, luminaries by day, this career woman–mother combo gig was great! When I sat down at the computer for the first time after childbirth, Theo was asleep in his Century car seat at my feet. And as "Lunching with D.C.'s Powerful" began to unfold, I remember gazing at sweet Theo and at the names of celebrities on my screen and thinking, "Oh, God, *I love my life*." My brain was no longer mush like the substances all around me that went in and out of Theo; the Cosmo Girl was making a comeback, stringing together power sentences just like Before Babe:

"Marilyn Quayle likes to do it at Germaine's." My words danced across the page. "Ron Brown does it at Mr. K's. Lee Atwater at Joe and Mo's or his Red, Hot and Blue. Brendan Sullivan does it at The Palm. George Will and Nancy Reagan used to do it at the Jockey Club. But for a true schmooze-'em-up, neck-craning Washington special, Duke Ziebert's gets raves above the rest."

By May, when Theo was four months old, I was sitting in a poolside bar at a Hyatt hotel in Sacramento interviewing Reza Pahlavi, the exiled son of the late shah of Iran. After his father died in 1980, Pahlavi had surfaced with the goal of becoming the umbrella symbol for all exiled Iranian nationalist groups, a move that riled the Islamic Khomeini regime to the point that the junior shah led their Most Wanted list. So we snuck around the capital of California surrounded by his bodyguards and heavy police detail, which was particularly thick on a walk through the park leading to the state legislature where Squeaky Fromme tried to pump a bullet into President Gerald Ford in 1975. The suspense and action was making me feel young and vigorous, out of the housefrau harness, back on the saddle of life.

You know what saddle I mean; the saddle on a galloping steed, his head high, eyes on fire. Not the saddle of the old nag you feel you're riding when you've just had a baby, the horse who keeps getting you caught in branches and brambles and ditches.

After a day of hiding out with Reza Pahlavi, I took a steamy bath at the Hyatt of Sacramento and slithered between the cool, fragrant sheets. As I was unwrapping the chocolate on my pillow and fantasizing about replacing Diane Sawyer on *60 Minutes*, I looked at the expanse of bed and realized it was the first time since Theo was born that he hadn't slept next to me. My breasts hardened, so I latched on to the electric Medela pump I had rented from the local La Leche League and called Chuck in a time zone three hours away. He answered in a whisper, telling me that Theo had fallen asleep on top of his chest and that he was going to sleep, too. From my deluxe suite overlooking palm trees that fluttered like giant emerald fans, my mouth full of dark chocolate caramel, I said good-bye to my boys in Washington, D.C., then dumped the six ounces of milk I had expressed into the toilet. I thought of the harshness of the breast pump compared to my baby's soft suckle. And when I picked up a yellow legal pad to organize my Pahlavi profile all I could do was sit and stare, submerged in visions of Theo in a snap-bottom undershirt with red ships on it, his little bare legs stretched across Chuck.

I didn't take an overnight business trip again until more than a year later, instead centering my journalism in Washington, writing an occasional piece for the Style section of the *Washington Post*, and becoming the staff writer for the city's art magazine, *Museum & Arts Washington*. Because of this position at the magazine, I was able to interview many leading artists, from Roy Lichtenstein to Annie Leibovitz. This visibility earned me a slot as a panelist on "Around Town," a weekly television program on Washington's PBS affiliate that spotlights cultural events in the capital.

Since I had been a fledgling reporter in my twenties doing food stories for the *Chicago Tribune*, my goal was to be on television. So when "Around Town" producer Jackson Frost called and invited me to become a commentator on this show that was watched by some forty thousand viewers weekly, I accepted in a warbling scream like you hear from finalists at the Miss America pageant. "Around Town" played back on Thursday nights at 8:30 P.M., and Theo, Chuck, and I would sit on the couch and watch me throw back my head and say smart things. My cheeks were flushed, my eyes popped out of sockets void of dark circles—all thanks to Roz, the station's wizard makeup artist. To comment intelligently on all the new plays and new museum shows and art gallery openings in Washington meant going to all the events. I would often take Theo, who by the time he was a year old was a regular at the National Gallery of Art.

We saw Rauschenbergs. De Koonings. O'Keeffes. Picassos. We watched the *Nutcracker* ballet at the Kennedy Center, plays on AIDS at street theaters. We stood together at the Phillips Collection in front of Auguste Renoir's *The Luncheon of the Boating Party*, one of the great, languid, flirty paintings of the world. Theo would laugh and laugh as he watched his mommy talking about high art on the same TV screen where Barney lived. But when "Around Town" was over he would always cry inconsolably, "Mommy gone! Mommy gone!," as if I had dis-appeared forever. His shrieks gave me such guilt, accusing me of something I knew I was doing—being there but not being there, making his life fit my life, not the other way around. I defended my fast rebound to the glamour-track by assuring my-self I was giving Theo culture at an early age, but this reasoning, of course, was ridiculous.

What babies want most are to be in their mother's arms and to have their mother's car keys in their mouth. This feeling of being two places at once, and not being either place very well, was augmented during a story I did for the July 1990 issue of *Life* magazine commemorating Rose Kennedy's one hundredth birthday. The assignment was to do a series of interviews with Kennedy family members about their memories of the matri-arch who had bolstered the clan throughout its proud and pain-ful history. After talking to sixteen Kennedys about bloodlines and loyalty and storybook moments with brothers and sisters and cousins and a grandmother who just wouldn't quit, I be-came newly convinced that the power of family can sustain you through everything. Bernice used to look at Chuck and me and Theo, shake her head, and say, "Nothin' like a family, I'll tell ya"—and she was right, as usual.

Or as Rose Kennedy herself once said of her guiding mission as a mother: "What greater inspiration and challenge are there for a mother than the hope of raising a great son or daughter?"

But the line that went the farthest to inspire me didn't even appear in the *Life* article. I had been trying to reach Ethel Ken-nedy at her home in McLean, Virginia, for several days, but she was always out or unavailable. Finally, just before deadline, the telephone rang and I heard "Hello, this is Ethel Kennedy." This woman I had been working so hard to reach was getting back to me precisely when I had a baby in my arms just rising from his nap who was shrieking into the receiver. And this mother of eleven said to me, "We can do this later. You go do what's really important."

"You go do what's really important" echoed and echoed as I changed Theo's diaper, put him to my breast, and turned on Oprah. It was late in the afternoon and instead of feeling anxious about my *Life* piece, which was due in two days, I was content to be sitting, nursing, waiting for Chuck, wondering if Oprah Winfrey, one of the most famous people alive, wanted children. This was rare, to feel good about doing nothing, and not itching to be somewhere else. Not that I could have been anywhere else anyway: When your baby is hungry and wet and there's nobody else around, you've got to be where you are.

These I'm-at-One-with-the-Moments started to wash over me more often during new motherhood, twitters of calm when my mind would empty as I performed simple, necessary household chores. One came when I was scrubbing out stained baby bottles, a painstaking task that demands lots of wrist action with long-stemmed brushes, another when I was dicing Monterey Jack into Kraft elbow macaroni with a dull ivory-handled knife. Mesmerized by the movement in the second and minute, I would become the cheese, the knife, the curls of pasta in my Pyrex bowl. The mundane in the everyday was connecting me to the Zen I thirsted for in my youth, the Zen I wanted so, so badly when I read *Zen in the Art of Archery* by Eugen Herrigel long ago:

"This everyday mind is no more than sleeping when tired, eating when hungry. As soon as we reflect, deliberate, and conceptualize, the original unconsciousness is lost and a thought interferes.

"Man is a thinking reed, but his great works are done when he is not calculating and thinking. 'Childlikeness' has to be restored with long years of training in the art of self-forgetfulness," adds Herrigel.

Alas, however soothing was the self-forgetfulness that came from Being There Now, I remained on fast-forward when a sexy new assignment came my way, snapping me back into Being Where When and sprinting from place to place. A big part of me wanted to surrender to the macaroni and cheese in the oven bubbling away in the Corning Ware. But I could not yet say no to uncharted frontiers in journalism. I made more money freelance writing Theo's first year than I ever made working for a company. Obviously, there was still a need to prove that my edge had not disappeared.

How did all these other not-so-young mothers who were coming off full, fun lives do it? I'd meet these women at dinner parties who made it seem so effortless, moms who would laugh and converse and mill about a room while their babies slept fashionably in hip slings, attached to them like designer accessories. Babies as fashion statements was the first trend in a long time that I had no part in perpetuating. My idea of a great night out during Theo's first year was to sit alone at a sushi bar guzzling a big can of Japanese beer.

It was in the throes of identity upheaval that the August 20, 1990, issue of *People* came out with a picture of a gorgeous Connie Chung, then forty-three, on the cover with the headline: I WANT A CHILD. Over the course of twenty years of reporting, she had worked her way up to one of the top journalism jobs in America. But now Chung, the youngest of ten children, was cutting back her schedule as a CBS-TV anchor to take aggressive medical action as a last-chance effort to conceive with husband Maury Povich. Seeing Chung on that cover, her red nails toying with a strand of pearls, the smile of a winner, I reacted this way: I have what you want, but a hunk of me still wants what you have.

THE MILITANT MAMA

The full import of Ethel Kennedy's words—"You go do what's really important"—didn't hit me until months later. On the afternoon of January 26, 1991, I came home at 5 P.M. and Bernice was rocking Theo and singing him Jesus songs. She said he was "real sick," and that she had called Chuck, who was on his way home. Theo was real sick indeed; he had a temperature of 104, his lips were purple, and he was having chest retractions from labored breathing. By the time Chuck got to the pediatrician's office he was sent directly to the nearest hospital emergency room, where I met him. The diagnosis was severe croup. After watching my father's health spiral out of control from an artillery of drugs in a hospital, I was determined to be bolder when hit with another family health crisis.

The side effect of streptokinase for my father was that it killed him, and I vowed that I would never again be passive and ignorant about drugs given to loved ones. Chuck was great, he let me take charge, he knew that my aggressive questioning came from a medical disaster that had forever changed the way I treated doctors and their medicine.

As soon as we were admitted, a nurse rushed in with a syringe full of a steroid solution, and an inhaling mask pumping a condensation of adrenaline called epinephrine. She informed us that these two treatments were standard for shrinking the airway inflammation caused by the croup virus.

Shuddering at the word "standard" that had also been used by one doctor to describe streptokinase to treat heart attacks, I asked about the drugs' harmful side effects. We were informed that epinephrine can accelerate the heart rate, increase anxiety, and have a rebound effect, meaning that the benefits of the drug are short-lived and when the symptoms return they can actually be worse. But Theo was fighting to breathe, and we agreed with the nurse's orders: "Your baby needs this now!"

That incident set the tone for our entire eleven-day hospital stay. Armed with a pediatric textbook loaned to us by a medical student and a fat consumer's guide to drugs, we researched every medication and treatment administered to our baby. With Chuck as my support beam, my mothering and journalism instincts turned me into an indomitable force. "You go do what's really important" echoed within every second of the day and translated into "Fight for your child's life!" So when we noticed that after two days of epinephrine Theo's breathing was getting worse, not better, and that his heart rate was consistently more than 220 beats a minute—normal is 160—we asked that the drug be stopped. We were almost too late; that dread epinephrine had already rebounded to the point where Theo's airway was sealing off, his anxiety was skyrocketing, and he was choking for air. We called in an ear, nose, and throat specialist who told us that our son needed to be transferred immediately to the pediatric intensive care unit.

Imagine this: a thirteen-month-old child whose natural anxiety is enhanced by drugs staring up into the faces of four big strangers in white coats pushing his bed under harsh hospital lights. He can't see Mommy and Daddy, who are trailing behind. Our son was in such terror he went into respiratory failure, and was taken instead to the operating room where a clear plastic tube was inserted down his windpipe to hook him up to a respirator.

Oh, God, you took my father, please don't take my only son, I prayed and prayed while we signed forms that warned us that one of the possible side effects of general anesthesia and respirators is death. Our pediatrician, Dr. Frank Palumbo, stayed in the operating room throughout the procedure and when he came and got us his face was white: "Theo is in bad shape. He went into bronchial spasms and his lung collapsed during the procedure." On the ride up in the elevator to the intensive care floor where Theo was being taken, I passed out.

I awoke to smelling salts and to the news that our baby was alive and stable.

Over the next several days I learned more and more about what it means to be a Mother, the bearer and protector of life. I was the Militant Mama from hell who barraged doctors with questions, the mother who hid in the bathroom when the nurse walked through the room to tell parents that visiting hours were over, the mother who vowed to God if Theo lived I would change my career-bitten ways, the mother who laid on top of her child to block a nurse who wanted to give Theo a tranquilizer, even though he was sedate and breathing easy, adjusting well to his first day off the respirator. I am not a doctor, as I was informed dozens of times by doctors during our stay at the hospital, but I did know this: tranquil babies don't need tranquilizers.

I also know that when you are standing by your child's bed and he's sputtering for air because a mucus plug got caught in his breathing tube and the nurse shoves you out the door and shrieks for a doctor, who races in, yanks out the old tube and inserts a new one and saves your son from death by twenty seconds, that the essence of motherhood is instantly, completely, irrevocably, transformed. The true meaning of mother—A Person Who Must Pay Full Attention—was hammered home a thousand other ways while pacing the intensive care ward. I will never forget one woman who was sobbing because the rectum of her four-month-old baby was raw from the suppositories of medication he was being given several times a day—babies on respirators can't swallow anything. I suggested that she do as we did, ask the nurses to administer the drugs through the IV tube instead.

She looked at me blankly, then anger flashed through her tears: "I just figured they knew what they were doing," she began in a small voice, then she shouted: "But I am Patrick's mother, aren't I? I can tell them what I think." I answered: "Yes, we are their mothers and we can demand to be listened to. Our children's survival depends on it."

After doing battle with a respiratory virus compounded by drugs and hospital staff mistakes, Chuck and I felt as if we had been through a war, a war that had ravaged our psyches but at the same time left us with an extraordinary sense of empowerment. I felt more accomplished than I ever had in my life. Knowing that we fought our hearts out and collaborated with destiny to win our child back made everything else that had ever puffed my ego seem like drivel. You have not a clue about the expanse of your real capabilities until you are attempting to ward off the strong arm of death from your baby. I will forever be convinced that we saved Theo's life by taking charge of the dehumanizing, dangerous plight that hospitalization generally means, by Being There, with all our might. When we realized our twenty-nine-pound baby was being pumped with a dozen different drugs we finally said "enough," standing up to doctors and saying no to their prescriptions.

My dear father in his demise taught me a hard lesson about illness: Family members must be diligent patient advocates or else everybody loses in the end. I ended up feeling like a partner on the medical team in charge of my son's life rather than the enraged bystander I was for the grandfather he never met. When Theo finally began to recover, we made it clear that we wanted no medication given unless it was absolutely essential to treat an already existing problem. Those doctors who challenged me were told, "I am his mother and this is what I want." And, boy, were we certain we wanted Theo's massive drug menu to be diminished after watching the progress of other tiny patients in the pediatric intensive care unit. Of the four deaths in eleven days, three were catalyzed by bad reactions to drugs or invasive procedures. That Theo survived his hospital stay was a miracle in itself. To give you an idea of the pharmaceutical collision taking place in his body, he was on drugs that paralyzed him so he wouldn't yank out his breathing tube and at the same time he was on drugs that made his heart race and anxiety soar. You don't have to be a doctor to be dead sure that this kind of cross-drugging that flips on totally opposing systems can't be good for anyone.

On the freezing morning of February 10, 1991, we lifted our boy out of his hospital bed, plunked him in his red wagon nestled against Ernie and Barney, and left the hospital. But our plight wasn't over. The robust baby who said "Big Bird" and "Mama" and ran all over the house a couple of weeks earlier now would not walk or talk or smile. He wouldn't even pull Max the cat's tail, preferring to sit quietly, staring, sucking on me or a bottle. We were told that he could have Guillain-Barré syndrome, and that he should be evaluated by a neurologist. After fully researching this disease that hits nerve roots and can lead to respiratory failure, I came away convinced that our boy didn't have Guillain-Barré or any other weird illness. What Theodore Anthony had, just like his grandpa before him, was too many drugs overwhelming his system. It took five full weeks before Theo recovered from all the junk that had been poured into him.

What was clear during the foggy days in the hospital was that the parents who had more than one child tended to do better when hit with a pediatric emergency. Of course, this should be obvious, but having "an heir and a spare" is only a trite saying until you are there on the front lines of a medical disaster that involves your only child. To this day I need to brace myself against a wall when I think about the mother who gave birth to a baby the same day her two-year-old daughter in a room across the hall from Theo died from an adverse reaction to a drug after heart surgery. Six hours after delivery, this mom came to the pediatric intensive care unit to kiss her older daughter good-bye for the last time. I saw her weakly walk to the bedside, lean over the lifeless body, and put her head down on her little girl's small chest. She told us she was leaving to go nurse her new baby at a hospital in Virginia twenty minutes away.

Theo's illness did many things. I became guilt-ridden: Why hadn't I paid more attention to the barky cough and low-grade fever that was a precursor to croup? I became newly religious: Thank you, God, for saving our child. And I loved Chuck more than ever. But I did not change my career-bitten ways; one week after Theo came home I was sitting across from one of my long-standing heroes, photographer Annie Leibovitz, who had agreed to be our cover story for *Museum & Arts* magazine to coincide with an exhibition of her work at the National Portrait Gallery. While Theo was in the hospital, I had to postpone the interview twice. When I finally met with Leibovitz in her cavernous studio at the crossroads of Tribeca and SoHo, one of the first things she said was, "Do you have any pictures of your baby?"

So I did what I tell my journalism students at American University never to do: I prattled on about our kid when I should have been using every second to flush out my esteemed subject. But the time spent on Theo and Chuck led to the stuff that makes an interview good: Annie Leibovitz ended up talking about the profound impact her own five siblings made on her. Her take on the value of family made a far deeper impression on me than any of her anecdotes involving the famous people she had photographed.

When I was living in the Bay Area in the mid-1970s, Annie Leibovitz was twenty-six and the chief photographer at the San Francisco–based *Rolling Stone* magazine. She was single and cool and enormously successful, thick with rock icons like Mick Jagger and Jerry Garcia. As a journalism student enticed by celebrity and freedom, I watched her from the sidelines, awestruck by her power, her reach. That reach only became more expansive over the years: no baby boomer will ever forget the Leibovitz photograph of John Lennon curled up naked in a fetal position next to Yoko Ono, who was eerily, prophetically, clad in all black. That picture was taken on December 9, 1980, at their apartment in the Dakota hours before John Lennon was murdered outside the building.

Six feet of black jeans and a black turtleneck, the forty-one-year-old artist I met in her four-thousand-square-foot studio still proved to be someone who left me awestruck, but for reasons beyond her startling photography. Unknowingly, Annie Leibovitz reinforced the spirit behind Ethel Kennedy's "what's really important," and it wasn't from her covers for *Vanity Fair* or a talent that commands up to $10,000 a day. It would have been easy to be boggled by her résumé alone. While many of her high-octane subjects have run out of gas, and others, like John Lennon, Andy Warhol, and John Belushi, have died, she has remained America's premier eye on the reigning figures of popular culture, a feat that is not lost on her.

"You know, it's not like you don't ever get caught up in it," Leibovitz said. "I mean, you can be cool, but you can also be too cool. There's a difference. And with Bruce Springsteen, it's still like, 'Ohhh, here I am in Bruce's car and he's driving his Camaro in New Jersey,' and it's still a little exciting.

"But I don't go out to dinner with these people. They are not my friends. I don't talk to Bruce Springsteen between album covers."

Leibovitz considers her brothers and sisters her best friends, relationships she counted on while shuffling between military bases with an air force colonel father. By the time she entered Northwood High School in Silver Spring, Maryland, she had lived in Connecticut, Alaska, and Texas. So the gaggle of Leibovitz brothers and sisters were bound extremely close, a cushion of love, she said, that left her with unrealistic expectations: "As you get older, you try and figure out why you are the way you are," said Leibovitz, who never married or had children. "And one of those reasons is, yes, they were my best friends. And you didn't need anyone else. And worse than that, you now expect those things from your other best friends. And no one else can give it, that unconditional love."

My sister, Fran, seventeen months older than me, and I had always remained very close, no matter how much we disagreed over the years. I understand her completely; she knows me inside and out. Often I feel as if we share a heart. She told me that when our father died the blow was softened because she had a daughter, Marissa, whom she loved with the same fervor and wholeness as Theodore Krasnow had loved his own children. So I knew firsthand what Leibovitz was talking about when describing family sinew and unconditional love. I was curious to know whether she wanted her own children.

She started off by describing a frustrating stage she had gone through three years earlier in her career when she was "doubting everything," and felt stuck. She wanted to change her style, make it better, but was paralyzed by the enormity of the task. "I knew how much work was required to make my photography stronger, and I didn't know if I could do it. But it was in this plateau period that I did do it, I started taking a few more risks. And because of that, I feel like I moved into a better place.

"And it's been a big sacrifice," she continued. "I mean, I basically spend my whole life doing my work. It's really been an obsessive thing. I'd love to have children. I mean, I come from a large family. It was in my middle thirties when I suddenly said, 'Oh, I'd better start figuring this out.' And here it is, years later, and it's like, oops. But the work has been a full-time baby and it needs to be fed.

"I always thought if I just kept doing the work it would be good."

It's like, oops. It's like, oops. That line reverberated in my mind. It's like, oops, I missed my moment. I knew it was going but I was busy and now that moment is gone. And now, I can't get it back. On the two-and-a-half-hour Metroliner back to Washington, with the wails of Carole King's "It's too late baby now, it's too late" coming back to me, I thought about how I was right there, mothering in the moment, trying to keep Theo alive in the hospital. I thought about how distracted I often got while mothering him at home, rocking him on my knees while yammering away to a public relations officer from the National Gallery, trying to get information on an exhibit we were covering on the "Around Town" TV show. I thought about how that Christmas morning we brought newborn Theo home stuffed in a red flannel stocking seemed like yesterday but was really fourteen months ago, a period of time where my career was not only on track but had never been better. And how was Theo? Could he be better?

My work, like Annie Leibovitz's, had been a full-time baby that needed to be fed, and I had fed it and it had fed me, but I was still very hungry. Now I had a real baby: there was no question which baby should get the most food, which baby was feeding me the most. And I thought about how omnipotent I had felt during Theo's hospital stay, more powerful than I had ever felt interviewing celebrities who, like Leibovitz had experienced, were not true friends.

So what does matter? Who is my true self, and where does she belong? The central questions of my youth came back to haunt me. But unlike my twenties, when I would sift through philosophy books or gravitate toward new men for clues, I was starting to see that the answer was right there within reach. As I learned during the hospital ordeal with Theo—the toughest way you can learn it—all you have, really, ever, is the moment, a flicker of time that passes through your fingers like sand. If Theo had died in February 1991, we wouldn't even have had film footage of him. We had been putting off our purchase of a video camera because Chuck and I could never coordinate our jammed schedules to meet at a camera store and choose one together. The week Theo was released from the hospital we bought a Canon Camcorder and conceived Isaac Mason Anthony. And we vowed to change our lives, relax our pace, move to a rural spot on the water in Maryland, and make good on our vow of having four children before we were forty.

I envisioned myself in one of my old gypsy skirts sitting on a hill surrounded by four children, overlooking a river. I would have my face turned to the sun like the woman in the Maxfield Parrish's "Ecstasy" poster, surrendering, ecstatically, to the Higher Power of procreation, sort of like Letting Go and Letting God but more like Letting Go and Letting Children Take Over. Surrender would mean victory, not defeat. I would fall back into this clingy, crying mass of soft flesh and shout: "Yes, Yes, Yes, I am." I would not resent the loss of identity that being absorbed by a litter of kiddies would mean.

Surrender, surrender, as in I Give Up, take me, life, the white flag is waving. Surrender: "To yield to the higher power of another," is the definition in the *New Merriam-Webster Dictionary*. Annie Leibovitz surrendered to the enormous task of making her work better, and as she put it, "it's been a big sacrifice."

She reminded me of another gutsy woman of achievement I had interviewed for *Museum & Arts*, Zelda Fichandler, a mother of two sons who worked her entire adult life to create and build Arena Stage Theatre in Washington. Fichandler first planted the idea that I should let my career stall and instead flourish in the home during my child's first years. Driving along the Potomac River to Arena Stage, I felt tarty with Al Green blaring, "I'm so in love with you, can't help myself. . . ." I was not thinking about lying on the gray carpet at home with six-month-old Theo; I was thinking about being single on Wisconsin Avenue. When Fichandler told me I looked good for just having had a baby, I felt the way I always felt when people said that—ecstatic to be able to separate my two selves, grungy mother and glamorous journalist. As the glamorous journalist talking to Fichandler about how her career grew so huge I heard her wistfulness because she had not surrendered to the grungy mother phase that is swift to pass.

This response came after I asked her if she had any regrets in a remarkable life that spawned the first regional theater in the United States. The sixty-five-year-old Fichandler stared at me for a minute, her eyes black and piercing, then she said: "If I had a perfect life to live over again, I would spend the first five years of my children's lives at home. But at the time, I never felt guilty about leaving the kids. I kept feeling 'this is worth it.'

"Now I give advice to young women embarked on missions to be very careful whether it's worth it. I'm not absolutely positive now that it's been worth it. Because of life not lived, books not read, art not seen, vacations not taken, conversations not held, flowers not smelled."

Fichandler paused, then she added: "Yeah, there is an upside and a downside. I never had enough of my kids. I do feel that I was always there when they needed me. But I don't think I was always there when I needed them."

She was about to turn sixty-six, but rather than retreat to the lazy, warm womb of Florida like many of her retired friends and actually read some of those books she had missed in her zeal to catapult Arena Stage to the top, she was still climbing the ladder, having just accepted a post as artistic director of the Acting Company in New York City, training ground for performers of the caliber of Kevin Kline and Patti LuPone. It was an irresistible offer and she couldn't turn it down. It was evident to both of us that Zelda Fichandler was never going to stop, that she'd been wound up for so long it was impossible for her to wind down.

I couldn't forget some of her lines from that interview. They hounded me during the ride home from Arena Stage, then over the next couple of weeks while I was nitpicking over words in a dark office, trying to make my Fichandler story perfect when

I could have been strolling with Theo in the spring sun on a sidewalk lined with the season's first daffodils. Those lines stuck by me throughout the nine-month gestation of our second child, most of which I spent tracking Dan Rostenkowski and putting together a nine-thousand-word profile on the Illinois congressman for *Chicago* magazine. As I sat through tedious hearings on the Hill and flew back and forth to Chicago to trail him, five months, then six months, then seven months pregnant, Zelda Fichandler would come back to me—she, the mother of two adult sons who admitted that she didn't think she was always there when she needed to be around her children, to be hugged and to laugh in her home.

Here I was, thirty years younger than Fichandler, but I was already feeling that chunks of my life had passed me by. This was augmented by macho Rostenkowski, the father of four grown daughters, who scolded me for running around chasing news stories when I should have been at home waiting for my baby and taking care of the one I already had. I'd wonder if he was right.

Yet how could I step away from a mercurial career? When I'm a granny with a white ponytail snaking down my back I'll be able to sit down with my grandchildren and regale them with tales of old—reading the New Testament with Billy Graham at the Essex House on Central Park South, nibbling on peanuts with Queen Noor at her palace while her husband chewed out Yasir Arafat. I was riding on the edge and it was breathtaking. There was no husband, no babies, nothing but me, me, me.

As a journalist I was swept up in a revolving cast of characters, a merry-go-round that distracted me from having to deal with who I was. Who I Am and Who You Are is impossible to avoid when you live with one husband and one baby in one house. These people we are bound to by marriage and by blood possess us, they are all over us every day. And they are not going anywhere, so we are forced to confront our True Selves.

Surprisingly, I was starting to discover that I liked that person a lot.

In the months immediately following Theo's birth, Russia divided, Germany reunited, and America entered the Gulf War. As my colleagues covered these global events, I was instead living a life I had never really lived before, my own. My reporter friends were flying on government planes to Kuwait, and I was left behind to roam nearby Rockville, Maryland, in search of a green turtle swimming pool that converts into a sandbox. Yet what I found in my new, smaller sphere was a place similar to journalism, teeming with action and thrills. But something was very different. The joy ran deeper than anything I had ever experienced before.

I was riveted by a story in the June 1990 *Esquire* by David Frankel called "The Last Housewife in America: A Portrait of the Endangered Species." His subject, JoAnn Stewart, relished, rather than resented, being a mom and a cook and a cleaning lady and a wife. She said "Bye, honey" and rubbed her husband on the back when he left in the morning to go to his job at Procter & Gamble. She did all the ironing. She cleaned all the toilets, smiling in a picture kneeling over the bowl wearing yellow rubber gloves, her Pine Sol and Comet perched by her side. Stewart recalled the time at a Christmas party when a woman turned to her and said, "What do you do?" She told her that she stayed home with her two sons.

"It kind of sounds shallow," Stewart said. "It sounds Victorian. It sounds boring. But it's not. Not to me."

I did not share her verve when it came to buffing up the bathrooms, but I knew what she was talking about when it came to her boys. My work was becoming shallow; my child filled me up. So why couldn't I finally, after a twisted, endless journey, be a wife and a mother and be happy at that? It was everything I had ever wanted; why wasn't it enough?

Is it enough for you? What else could we want?

It was during this confusion that a proper, southern lady in her late fifties gave me *The Adventures of Being a Wife* by Ruth Peale. Written in 1971 as the Women's Liberation movement was making young females balk at the chains of marriage, Peale's basic message was that marriage is the greatest career a woman can have, the greatest adventure of all, so Take Care of Your Man and Make Him Smile. It seemed to be working on her guy: Husband Norman Vincent Peale, author of *The Power of Positive Thinking*, appeared to be feeling good all the time. I smirked at the title and thought the premise of the book was archaic and sappy, but once I started reading I found Mrs. Norman Vincent Peale had some sobering things to say.

"I consider myself to be one of the most fortunate women alive," she writes. "Why? Because I am totally married to a man in every sense of the word: physically, emotionally, intellectually, spiritually. We're so close you couldn't put a knife blade between us."

So marriage was the greatest of all adventures, and not the cessation of all adventures as it often seemed to be. "We're one integrated organism, not two competing individuals," Mrs. Peale had boasted. Hmmm, integrated, as in whole, as in one. When I married Chuck I was thirty-three and he was thirty-one. After all that time being out there alone, we were still two ones standing apart in our new marriage, not meshed in bliss like the Peales. I was worried about my career, he was worried about his career, we both thought the other was doing less around the house, and we each needed perky Cincinnati housewife JoAnn Stewart to organize our lives.

But late at night, no matter how intense the skirmish of the day, we fell together as a family, Theo between us, under our green down comforter. Since the day he came home from his croup saga in the hospital I wanted him next to me so I could monitor his breathing while he slept—which he didn't do much. Other mothers swore by *Solve Your Child's Sleep Prob-*

lems, a tough guide by Dr. Richard Ferber that basically says endure the crying instead of picking babies up, and they will train themselves to sleep. But all I was interested in reading was Tine Thevenin's *The Family Bed: An Age Old Concept in Child Rearing* released in 1976 when hippies were growing up and wildly reproducing. This is the book that claims it's natural and healthy for human families to sleep as a group, that it actually gives children a better sense of security. I would hold Theo tightly, his back arched against my chest, my face in his curls, loving him fiercely.

His brother Isaac was born on November 23, 1991, by emergency cesarean section at Columbia Hospital for Women, after five hours of hard labor revealed a baby in breech position. When we brought our second son home, Theo didn't get to sleep next to Mommy for one of the first times in his life. He was outraged, a state that was fanned by another loss: I had weaned him the month before, and now Isaac had claimed me. Isaac's first day at home was on Thanksgiving. Bernice was off, and it was madness. My incision was killing me, and both boys were planted on top of it. Chuck and I looked at each other in a daze, slowly shaking our heads.

What had we done? Whose idea was this four before forty plan? We started fighting constantly, over how much time Chuck was spending at the office, over how tired I was of being stuck at home, over how babies had taken over our lives. My husband's grandmother Mattie Anthony had more kick at eighty-seven than I did at thirty-seven. To give you a sense of the mayhem in my mind, one late afternoon a couple of weeks after Isaac's arrival I started sobbing at the grocery store. Here's what set me off. As I groped for my wallet to pay the cashier I stumbled first upon a plastic Ernie holding three pastel balloons, then a book of green matches with the name of an Arabic restaurant at which I had dined while in Amman with a man named Ali from Queen Noor's office. The clashing symbolism of these two objects mirrored a clashing life of old ambitions and young sons. I thought about what it meant to surrender, that maybe I wasn't ready.

When the profile of Dan Rostenkowski appeared in the November 1993 issue of *Chicago* magazine, the attention it got sent me back on a familiar ego rush. I felt good about my story, entitled "Power Drive," on the gruff and combustible Chicago legend who, at the time I did the piece, was still King of the Hill as chairman of the omnipotent Ways and Means Committee, which controls a trillion and a half dollars in federal tax, trade, and health-care revenues. The House of Representatives mailroom scam investigation that would lead to his seventeen-count indictment and eighteen-month prison sentence had not yet begun. But the part of the piece I kept reading over and over wasn't about the perks of Power Driving; it was the portion when the blustery patriarch of a family of four daughters talked about the toll he thought his workaholism had taken on his family.

In the thirty-three years that Rostenkowski had been in Washington, his wife, LaVerne, and their children had stayed in Chicago. To keep up with his marriage, his kids, his Washington schedule, and his speaking engagements, Rostenkowski took nearly two hundred plane trips a year. But despite the schizophrenic life and his approaching sixty-fifth birthday, he was still locked in the perpetual motion of his youth—reaching, running, toward what?

"I don't know what drives me," Rostenkowski said in a gravelly voice. "Well, I think there's a certain amount of pride in wanting to do what's necessary to get things done. I want to enjoy the comforts of my family, and I want to do my job here."

When I asked him if he felt he had succeeded in his joint mission, Rostenkowski answered in a soft and sad voice. "There's no question that I think I've met my public obligation," said the man who was instrumental in overhauling America's entire tax code under President Reagan. "Whether I've met my family obligation as well as I should have, I don't know." He stared in silence. "LaVerne raised those children. LaVerne has been the hub of the family."

It's been a family racked with woe. Three of his daughters are divorced; two have been arrested for cocaine possession. One of his best friends told me how Rostenkowski has cried late at night over martinis because he believes he has failed them. And at the age of sixty-four, it was too late to go back and try again—his girls were adults. I thought of Willy Loman, the tragic hero of Arthur Miller's *Death of a Salesman*, who worked a lifetime to pay off a house, and when he finally owned it, his kids were grown and, disgruntled with their family life, had moved out.

You marry, have children, make money, the children leave, the house is paid for but it is lifeless, an empty shrine to the should-haves in your life. Dan Rostenkowski clearly had pangs about missing things at home while he was ascending the ranks in Washington. I can't conclusively tell you it would have made any difference for his kids if he had, instead, run a family restaurant in Chicago and hired every Rostenkowski to work there, under one roof. No one can. While some child-rearing educators insist that extended absences by a mother or a father can do big damage to a child's self-esteem and ability to bond, others say your kids can still thrive under the charge of a solid, attentive caregiver, or in a single-parent home. Ultimately, figuring out what you and I can do to help our children succeed has to come from within.

When I listened to all the prescriptions from behaviorists, social theorists, psychoanalysts, and pediatricians on how to be a parent, I ended up feeling insecure and confused. My advice after muddling around for a while is to pick the ones who speak directly to you, and use them as a supplement to what you feel like doing. Some of those experts will agree that you should respect your own judgment even if it means ignoring theirs.

"Trust yourself. You know more than you think you do," Dr. Benjamin Spock told parents in his then revolutionary *Baby and Child Care* published more than fifty years ago, the first book to depart from the rigidity in child rearing that prevailed in postwar American culture. As Dr. Spock continued: "Don't take too seriously all that the neighbors say. Don't be overawed by what the experts say. Don't be afraid to trust your own common sense."

With two toddlers in tow, I was rapidly learning that my gut was the most valuable guide to follow, that you can't parent from the brain, you've got to parent from the soul. This can hurt—when your children act out, they are often holding up a mirror to you. Along with your gut and soul and Dr. Spock, pay attention to another long-ruling maven of motherhood, Penelope Leach:

"If your three-or four-year-old bites, hits, kicks, attacks younger children, pockets other people's toys and generally makes it impossible for anyone to like him for a playmate, look to his life at home," Leach writes in her bible to new parents, *Your Baby & Child: From Birth to Age Five.*

Penelope Leach is painfully on target when she tells us that, as parents, we reap what we sow. Look in your own play groups and living rooms, and you will see that depressed and indecisive mothers often turn out sad and explosive children. You will see that confident and consistent mothers often turn out confident and even-keeled kids. Children get their cues from watching how their parents act. I know in our home when my mood is molten everyone is volcanic. When I give in to a screaming child, he thinks I'm a pushover and screams even louder the next time he wants something. When we waffle, they waffle.

As new mothers, we come to realize quickly that setting a virtuous example as much as is humanly possible is our key responsibility as a parent. From this springs a next generation that respects authority and respects itself, our gift of hope and love to the earth we share, an "exercise of a fundamental generosity," as author Gabriel Marcel calls the act of childbearing. Virtuous qualities in offspring are tough to inspire when you're not around much to demonstrate them. Time with our children enlarges our virtue, too. Those sons and daughters gazing up at us for direction keep us honest.

One afternoon I came home from meetings in Washington and found Theo and our baby-sitter both in tears. He had been playing on the swing set and refused to come into the house when she asked him to. So this 105-pound woman dragged our 64-pound, five-year-old son through the grass, across the sidewalk, up the stairs, and through the front door. I sat Theo down on the couch and asked him what happened.

"Mommy, I missed you," he said between sniffles. "I climbed on top of the monkey bars so I could watch for your car coming. It was taking too long. You said you'd be home in an hour."

I thought back to when I was leaving that morning and remembered that I did indeed tell him I'd be gone "about an hour." He held me to my word, as he should, even when I had knowingly fudged the truth so that I could get out of the house without a big separation scene. And when I didn't come through for him as promised, he lost it. I admitted my mistake to Theo and told him that I was not perfect, and that every day I try to be a better person than I was the day before. I also reminded him that it's the baby-sitter's job to keep him safe when I'm not there and that means he has to do what she says.

That night in bed I pictured Theo perched atop the monkey bars staring down the empty driveway, waiting, watching, wishing his mother's blue Suburban would come toward him so he could leap down, race toward her, and jump into her arms. What I didn't tell my son was that I, too, was in tears because

I was stuck in a ninety-five-minute traffic snarl from Washington to Annapolis, all the while thinking of the children I was missing at home.

Some women admit outright that they can't stand being around their kids for hours at a time. It makes them tense and anxious, angry, even bored. These mothers would be doing their children no favors by staying home. But most working moms anguish over what to do: They love being with their children, but they also crave and need the excitement of a job, and often the money that comes along with it. The few hours a week I spend in Washington teaching a journalism course and meeting with editors are liberating and invigorating and lucrative. Yet I often worry about how much time away from the kids is too much for them or not enough for me.

I asked Theo and Isaac's preschool director, Ellie Martin, if she had witnessed any definitive behaviors during her eighteen years on the job, an era that saw a proliferation of dual-career parents leading frenzied lives and the advent of the nanny generation. After working with hundreds of children and their families, representing a broad range of backgrounds, this was her primary observation:

"In the end, what kids need the most is knowing they can really depend on somebody else to be there to take care of them," says Martin. "And when they don't feel like they have that, they've got to push the boundaries all the time, testing how far they can go, as if they are really asking 'When is somebody going to save me from this? Who's going to catch me?'

"Hopefully, a lot of nannies can handle the job, but I think there is really that overall sense by children that it's their parents they will respond to the best and it's their parents who they are connected to the most."

With no Child Czar and no study out there preaching the absolute right way to go on this universal trigger issue for parents, how to merge career and children can only be gauged by the compass in our hearts, that magnetic intuition that tugs toward a choice that is right. To steady this seesaw of job and kids, it is crucial to try and figure out what lies at the source of your professional desires, especially if you're like me, drawn to the workplace predominantly by ego and a need to create and not by monetary rewards. From this exercise can emerge a re-defining of the words "need" and "want."

Do you need All That Job, or could you live with less power and less money? Can you cut back to part-time, like my lawyer friend Sandy Kalter, the mother of two young boys? She went off partner track at her firm to a thirty-two-hour week and is home every night for dinner, doesn't work weekends, and no longer takes travel assignments.

Do you, too, need, Right Now, to spend more time with your children? What is driving you the hardest? What do you want the most? Is it time to transfer your business to the home?

When I turned to my heart for lucidity on my own drive I saw a woman whose sense of worth had always been deter-mined by her accomplishments. I had to be the best, and I worked very hard to make that happen: If my editor suggested talking to ten people for an article, I'd find thirty. I labored for hours over writing the perfect lead paragraph. When sources I had to get to didn't return my calls, I tracked down their ap-pointments and stood in front of them as they were entering or departing their meetings. Winning was everything. And for bet-ter or worse, I knew this wasn't going to disappear. But I heard something else from that voice within: "There are huge achieve-ments to be had at home, let your ambitions and creativity fly with those boys."

Becoming a good journalist requires intense energy and devotion. Becoming a good mother takes at least the same com-mitment, if not more—of this I was becoming certain. To suc-ceed, I would have to work harder than I'd ever worked on anything in my life, and that would mean stripping away as many peripheral distractions as possible. And I had to succeed, this had to be my finest hour—there was too much riding on it. I had only one chance to get it right.

A sense that the best place to devote the bulk of my time was at home with young children was reinforced by watching the families closest to me. Most of the sons and daughters of my friends who worked fifty-plus hours a week and had terrific child care generally seemed adjusted and content. It's their mothers who were rarely adjusted and content, having to stretch themselves so taut that they felt as if they'd snap any second. When they were at the office they couldn't wait to be home; when they were at home they were worried about getting behind at work. They constantly complained how there was so much to do they weren't able to do anything well.

Living in guilt and conflict, while setting yourself up for failure because no person alive can do everything all at once, is not any way to be. That's not living, that's suffering. You can't win this tug-of-war without letting go of one side of the rope.

THE SURRENDER

Work, work—I've got work to do. Hadn't that been my own motto, my own mission, to achieve and achieve and achieve? Was it really time to halt in my tracks for Theo, Isaac, and Chuck? But if I did that, then what? Journalism was Who I Am.

I remembered my own mother headquartered in her home in the mid-1960s, and how I used to watch her whip through the house, lining things up, making things perfect. My thought was: This woman could have been somebody; instead, she's wasting all that talent on housework and us. What I didn't realize at the time was that she was already somebody, somebody major, the biggest thing she could ever be: a mom who structured our days and gave us stability. But in my naive youth, all I saw in my home were sexist roles, sending me and my generation of women far away from the kitchen to find ourselves.

We traveled wide and labored long to establish Our Jobs, Our Lifestyles, Our Things—the idea of peeling away these layers, our glisteny armor, is scary. Without a Lifestyle, we'd be left only with a Life, and is that enough?

There is a wonderful Koren cartoon that appeared in *The New Yorker* depicting a young man in a sun visor, tennis racket at his feet, leaning against his Porsche Turbo parked at a beachfront resort with palm trees. His girlfriend, grinning idiotically, sits in the front seat in dark glasses and a floppy hat and a low-cut sundress. The fellow is telling a couple who are similarly garbed: "I despise my life, but I'm in love with my lifestyle."

The moral is obvious: His lifestyle is vacuous. Yet it's hard to suddenly make all the superficial trappings of success disappear, even if they leave you spiritually empty. Losing something that has been the long-standing center of your life means losing what defined who you are. Without these things you are then left with You, and who is that? For me, motherhood was the state in which I would have that revelation.

I had done a story for the May 1989 issue of *Self* magazine on yuppies throwing over big careers for more soulful vocations. But what my sources were telling me then didn't really sink in— I was having too much fun engulfed by my big career. When I went back to this article years later with a little boy on each knee, I got very excited about the prospect of re-creation of Self, of being reborn along with my sons. It was Kierkegaard who told us "Spirit is Self," and when you realize that your spirit is fluid and moldable and capable of becoming any Self you want to be, it's a reverberating wake-up call.

"What Do You Do for an Encore?" was the title of my story, for which I interviewed midlife professionals beaten down by jobs that had once charged them, and who had taken bold leaps in markedly different directions. Socked with constant headaches as a prosecuting attorney in Seattle, Linda Walton started a llama pack trip company in the North Cascade Mountains. Stuffed into the subway on hot New York afternoons, securities broker Don Steinman yearned to be unencumbered far away from the crowds. So he became a cowboy-rancher in Tucson, Arizona. Dick Caples was an associate with the law firm of Shearman & Sterling in New York City, wheeling in a global playground as a specialist in transactions between banks and international corporations. Lured by a love of the arts, Caples left law on the cusp of a six-figure salary to become executive director of the Lar Lubovitch Dance Company.

The unifying force that led this diverse group to shuck their old careers was spiritual discontent, as summed up by Caples, thirty-nine. In his new post as director of the nonprofit modern dance troupe that performed all over the world, he loved being able to work in blue jeans in a Bohemian loft in Chelsea, having moved from a starchy law office in Wall Street's Citicorp tower.

"The whole purpose of why I'm working, the raison d'être of my job, has completely changed," Caples told me. "Essentially, the practice of law was lacking emotional and psychic satisfaction. Only in the arts have I been able to feel that my life has greater purpose than merely helping a client make more money. I wanted to be in a job that was actually moving people, touching people in their deepest selves, that was working toward something that would be permanent and immortal."

Moving people, touching people in their deepest selves, working toward something that would be permanent. Who didn't want those things? All I had ever wanted was to connect with people, to have intimate relationships that came from Truth. And here, the opportunity was mine, Right Here, Right Now, I Had It All. With Theo and Isaac, I was given the chance to move mountains, to shape two people, to give them a foundation that would make them whole, to respond to their wonder, to teach them how to love. "I did not ask for success; I asked for wonder. And You gave it to me," Hasidic author Abraham Joshua Heschel wrote in the preface to his book of Yiddish poems, a volume that serves as his homage to God for all the miracles he had witnessed.

I had experienced success on the job; now I had wonder from children that were mine, connective tissue to a future of Being Touched in My Deepest Self, a link to my ancient Jewish roots. I think of the first time Theo saw his brother Isaac in the hospital. He crept in the door slowly, his daddy close behind, and he stopped in front of the plastic bassinet on wheels holding a sleeping, swaddled Isaac. Theo's eyes registered confusion, sadness, then landed on me with outright rage. I felt a tantrum coming on, but instead he broke out in the biggest grin. "Theo's baby," he said, then again, "Theo's baby," and again louder, "Theo's baby." He was shouting and laughing and poking the plastic near Isaac's tiny head. "Theo's baby. Theo's baby. Theo's baby," he kept up his chant. Watching his wonder with the most precious blessing of all, the birth of a child, is still a touchstone of joy for me nearly four years later. When a child discovers the world, that enchantment is so pure you pray he will retain that wonder throughout a lifetime; it makes you feel innocent yourself.

While this supreme source of fascination does come from observing our children observing life, for so long I had also counted on journalism to fortify my Self, indeed, even to be my barometer of Self. However badly I wanted to make the leap, could I really make the necessary shift of the psyche to The Home from The World? "I asked for success, You gave me wonder," Heschel sings his praises to God. But, hey, how about combining wonder from children and worldly success—can't a mother have both? After seventeen years of being a writer first, and everything else second, this was going to be a difficult transition—taming a textbook Type A into a domesticated animal. How do you rid yourself of the itch that propelled you to the top in the first place? I was beginning to realize that you don't have to, that the next step forward for a Type A tiger could be as a focused Fierce Mama.

I thought of the plot of *Baby Boom*, the sugary, implausible movie with Diane Keaton as the Tiger Lady who graduates first in her class at Yale, gets her M.B.A. at Harvard, becomes a six-figure advertising executive, then inherits a baby from an English cousin she barely knows. She then leaves Manhattan, moves with daughter Elizabeth to a sixty-two-acre farm in Vermont with orchards and a pond, starts an instantly successful organic baby food company called Country Baby, and falls in love with Sam Shepard, a local veterinarian. I sat rapt watching Diane Keaton's second act in midlife with the sensational-looking Mr. Right she landed this time around. I wanted to be Diane in the Vermont woods, her baby girl slung around her hips, Sam Shepard slung God knows where, mashing organic fruits and vegetables into baby food from produce she grew herself. I wanted to be that mother of the woods and of the sky and of my babies' flesh.

I started baking zucchini bread again, something I had not done since 1975 at Synergy House. I started making spaghetti sauce from scratch. I started saying "Hi, honey" to Chuck when he came home from work, and giving him a little rub on the back. I became a subscriber to *Welcome Home*, a magazine for the "smart woman who has actively chosen to devote her exceptional skills and good mind to the nurturing of her family," or so reads its mission statement. And just as domesticity was beginning to feel right, that damn issue of *Time* came out with Susan Faludi and Gloria Steinem on the cover, sounding "The Call to Arms" to fight the backlash against feminism. They were dressed in black and they looked strong and serious and, worst of all, skinny. It was March 9, 1992, Isaac was three months old, Theo was two, and I was about as prepared to join the call to arms as I was to go back to Sausalito and be hypnotized by the roll of whitecaps on the ocean and Jerry Garcia. But there they were, Faludi and Steinem, beautiful and cerebral, "reviving the revolution."

And where was I as feminism, once surefooted and surging forward, was left staggering? Drizzling baked apples with honey. I felt like a weak traitor, a player in the backlash they were talking about. Wasn't I one of those burnt-out superwomen fueling the backlash against feminism? I was embarrassed to tell my Stanford roommate Amy Rudnick, among the top legal experts on money laundering in America, as she told me of her trip to Panama to meet with the country's vice-president and attorney general, that my coup of late was finally locating the plastic tumblers with watermelons at Kitchen Bazaar I'd been looking everywhere for—perfect for backyard entertaining.

The old flip-flop Self was back, the woman chomping to charge ahead and the woman gratefully sedated by the kids weighing her down. It was the Self of age twenty described by Ram Dass I had tried to ditch back in Palo Alto—"like a yo-yo, I keep going up and coming down, up down, down, up down." Only at thirty-seven, I was starting to see that a yo-yo was what I may always be, and that wasn't bad or even rare for that matter. The thrust of nearly all my conversations with other working mothers was the ping-ponging emotions brought on by professions and children and marriage and the mashing of all of them together. It's okay to be a yo-yo, that's how you grow.

Teased by the *Time* piece on feminism, I was compelled to buy Susan Faludi's book *Backlash: The Undeclared War Against American Women*. As I started this work by a Pulitzer Prize–winning reporter who was younger and smarter than me, I found myself in a jealous snit. She was a sharp writer and clear thinker who held her own for 460 pages. I used to write for some of the finest publications on the stands, but now I was having trouble stringing five sentences together for baby-gift thank-you notes. Yet as I moved through *Backlash*, Faludi dissipated the envy with a poignant message targeted to worn-out Wonder Women. This firebrand author who had not yet married or had children was telling us: Don't blame feminism for all that ails you; bashing each other just sets us all back.

In years past, as an ascending and lonely public relations executive in Chicago, then as an ascending and lonely journalist in Dallas and Washington, I had often attributed my alienation with the disparate parts of my soul to growing up confused by the flood of choices borne by Women's Liberation. The inflamed writings of Betty Friedan and Germaine Greer and Simone de Beauvoir gave my generation both the drive to succeed and the curse of feeling cowardly guilt should we at some point decide to renounce the climb. So, rising high in my career was satisfying for two reasons: My sense of self-worth burgeoned along with my achievements, and I felt aligned with the feminist cause. Yet after years of doing right for my gender I often felt as if I wasn't doing right by me. Where should individual happiness fit into feminism? Of this I was never sure, not when I was a serial dater and hacking out a name for myself in journalism, and not as a newlywed bent on madly reproducing. Reading *Backlash* in the spring of 1992, at a standstill in my profession but mushrooming in the hearth, I began to feel very sure about how feminism and I fit together, that standing apart didn't weaken the bond.

As Faludi writes: "To blame feminism for women's 'lesser life' is to miss entirely the point of feminism, which is to win women a wider range of experience. Feminism remains a pretty simple concept. . . . The meaning of the word 'feminist' has not really changed since it first appeared in a book review in the *Athenaeum* of April 27, 1895, describing a woman who 'has in her the capacity of fighting her way back to independence.'

"Feminism's agenda is basic: It asks that women not be forced to 'choose' between public justice and private happiness. It asks that women be free to define themselves—instead of having their identity defined for them, time and time again, by their culture and their men."

And that was it. Terse and right on. Just what I needed to hear. Even though I had downshifted in my profession, I remained a committed feminist, empowered by my choice to be a mother at home, cranked up on coffee and kids. It was both my public justice and private happiness—for now at least. I did not want to be judged by women with babies who retained their full-time office jobs and thought I sold out; I did not want to be judged by housewives who considered themselves more hands-on mothers than me, women who had no help with their children and no help with the cleaning. Bernice helped me with both, and I knew how lucky we were. My only real disappointment with Faludi was that she snubbed the movie *Baby Boom*, deriding its heroine for what she felt was antifeminist behavior. She points to the scene where the Tiger Lady rejects a buyout offer of three million cash for Country Baby from one of her old corporate accounts.

"She could have spoken up for the rights of working mothers," insisted Faludi. "But instead, the former Tiger Lady's talk dribbles off into a dewy-eyed reverie about the joys of rural living. The last shot shows her back at home in a rocking chair, baby in her arms, surrounded by curtain lace and floral upholstery."

I was left thinking that Susan Faludi would like this scene better once she holds her own kid in a rocking chair, especially if it's a glider like the one we have, all cushy and comforting with its red padded seat and matching footstool. Wendy Wasserstein's Pulitzer Prize–winning play *The Heidi Chronicles* ends with its overachieving star, a political activist turned internationally acclaimed art expert, snuggling her newly adopted daughter from South America in a rocking chair in the middle of an empty apartment she has just moved into. Heidi was going at motherhood solo; of the two big loves of her life, one married someone else and the other turned out to be gay. Rocking her baby, Heidi appears to be satisfied for the first time in the play.

And why not? It doesn't get much better. Any driven woman who has been locked in perpetual motion for too many years will attest to the pure joy of sitting still and soothing her baby and herself with the sway of a rocking chair. I love that red rocker that Chuck surprised me with when Theo was born. As someone who had spent a lifetime chasing the ultimate feel-good experience in any country I could get to, I was stunned to discover the best sensation I could have was right within the length of my arms. Nothing ever felt so fine as having a small child slumped against my chest, rocking in the rhythm of the Now. Not journalism, not drugs, not the NordicTrack, not the Washington Power Game. Exalted in my red-cushioned throne, Theo and Isaac snoozing on top of me, my brain would drain and I'd feel giddy and light, floating in the second. Oh, Ram Dass, I'm still grasping, but I'm getting closer, closer, almost there, to that "trusting, open, surrendered, being" you speak of in *Be Here Now*, the one who finally melts into cosmic consciousness.

"Consciousness equals energy, love, awareness, light, wisdom, beauty, truth, purity. It's all the same trip," he writes. "The mindless quality of total involvement that comes only when the ego is quiet. . . . It is only when you reside quietly in your own Hridayam [spiritual heart] that you become He of total Light Unbearable Compassion and Infinite Power."

Unbearable Compassion? Infinite Power? Hail Ram Dass! This could be my trip at last, thanks to my babies. After splintered years of climbing and chaos, I was coming to know who I was, who I wanted to be, what I was best at, what made me the happiest. And it all came down to loving my boys, and the love I was getting back. From the battery pack of motherhood comes enlightenment, wholeness, the ongoing heat of passion.

Unquestionably, these children make me feel like there's an eternal flame within. But letting go of less soulful professional endeavors did not happen without a few hard-won setbacks and internal scuffles. Despite the Nirvana of the Red Rocker, I found myself saying yes again to producer Jackson Frost when he invited me on the TV show "Around Town." The pregnancy pounds were beginning to drop and I couldn't pass up the chance to join the witty, urbane cast of art critics watched by thousands of viewers in the Washington area on prime-time TV. With red lip-liner and mauve-dusted eyes, the glamour girl was briefly resurrected. But sometime during the half-hour taping— it never failed to happen—as my mouth would be clacking, my mind would be stuck on those two babies at home with Bernice. I envied other working mothers who told me how great it felt to leave the house in the morning and Have A Real Life apart from the children.

"It makes me such a better mother when I get home," they claimed. "Because I've done something for Me all day." I was not this animal. I had a three-hour internal time bomb that started ticking the second I closed the front door. If I left home at 9 A.M., by noon the alarm would detonate in my heart, and I'd become rattled by an urgency to see Theo and Isaac. When I was away, I called Bernice every half hour, and if she didn't answer I pictured the house burning down, or that she had fainted and Theo was gnawing on the top of a tube of toothpaste that was about to get lodged in his throat. Then who would do the Heimlich maneuver?

Once, when we were delayed at the WETA-TV studio to retape the opening of the show and my clock was going off, I nearly walked off the set, my innards were such a mess. Instead, I sat there, trying to relax into the moment by reciting my mantra from Transcendental Meditation. Sitting on a television stage in black high heels yearning to be down and dirty in a pile of kids, I realized that it was in my control not to be fractured and frantic. I was no longer the grinning high school cheerleader who had yet to become a True Self. I was finally somebody else, wholly somebody else. As I commented on the luminous work of Willem de Kooning at the National Gallery, the real Lights in My Soul were my children back home in the living room. It started to feel as if Me of Truth belonged in a sloppy and slobbery house, not in a museum. That shift became apparent.

There is a segment on "Around Town" when panelists get to recommend anything they want. And as my colleagues would cite things such as a new Italian film about lesbian teenagers I would inevitably hype an event for kids, like the Peter and the Wolf puppet show at Glen Echo Theatre or a coloring book of the Great Works of Art available at the National Gallery book-store. After years of keeping an eye on an international scope of news, it was a relief to shift my focus to the local, little things that were mine to have and to hold.

Relief, as in pulling on your sweats and letting that leg hair grow. Relief, as in the "lightening of something oppressive," as defined by *Webster's*. It was around this time that I delivered the keynote speech for the annual Metropolitan Area Mass Media Awards in Washington. I had won an award the year before for my *Museum & Arts Washington* profile of Zelda Fichandler. The event is a breakfast and awards ceremony that attracts many of the leading local print and broadcast journalists in the city. When I sat down to write my address there was a clutch in my belly: what could I offer this formidable group? While they worked the White House and Capitol Hill, I was sandpapering my kids' swing set so they wouldn't get splinters.

That morning in May I cleaned myself up so there wasn't a Similac spot in sight, no peanut butter in my hair, and I told the audience of distinguished journalists how Zelda Fichandler had made an impact. I recounted the interview with the founder of Arena Stage Theatre who admitted, "If I had a perfect life to live over again, I would spend the first five years of my children's lives at home," how she felt she was always there when her two boys needed her, but that she wasn't always there when she needed them. I talked about the glory days of UPI, interviewing Billy Graham and Queen Noor and Norman Mailer and Ted Kennedy, and the long nights swigging beer and swapping Inside Washington gossip with journalist pals at the Childe Harolde. Then I got to the struggle of my heart:

> Today, as the mother of two babies, writing is no longer the dominant force in my life, my family gets the most of me. Yet because I feel compelled to do

what Zelda Fichandler says she regrets she didn't do hardly makes it the right choice, or the better choice. Every woman should be able to choose what is right for her based on her own emotional and financial needs without getting slammed by society, or feeling resentment from her friends on different tracks.

We must respect each other's choices, and realize that for a mother to decide to work full-time or for a professional woman to opt to stay home are equally difficult, painful decisions laden with trade-offs. Let's hope these times will see a decline in name-calling; no more charges that the new hausfrau is antifeminist, or that the female careeraholic is busting her biological clock.

There is no us and them: we are all one body of women just trying to keep it together, career, family and personal growth. Those twenty-one women running for the United States Senate this year stand for all of us.

My opinion on what is better or right for professional mothers would become more hard-line as I had more children, but this is what I felt at the time.

I told them that my own decision to move from the newsroom to the nursery had some painful repercussions, that my competitive streak had far from vanished. I admitted that I had longed to be part of the pack covering the fallout over Clarence Thomas and Anita Hill, and the attempt to overturn *Roe* v. *Wade*. While big, breaking news stories were happening, like the ozone layer vanishing and Japan pulling out ahead of the United

States in industry, I laughed that I was at home eating Rice Krispies Treats and watching one of my favorite movies of all time, *Willy Wonka and the Chocolate Factory*.

"It gets really bad sometimes, this crush of anxiety," I admitted. "Although I'm proud of fellow journalist Susan Faludi, and her ability to research and compile the best-selling *Backlash: The Undeclared War Against American Women*, her success also makes me wince: Will I ever do anything that important in my life? Or, eeee God, have I peaked?"

In the end, I told them how thankful I was for an exciting career, for all my bylines on profiles in slick magazines. But that I would forever regret not stopping my pursuit of famous subjects long enough to run a tape recorder with my father—the most insightful and humorous person in the world. I wondered aloud if perhaps the most important thing I would ever do, my Personal Best, would be to raise good children.

People clapped long and loud, and after the breakfast was over, I was swarmed by women, both young journalists and senior citizen members of the American Association of University Women, the group that sponsored the awards. They all had stories.

A TV anchorwoman got teary when she relayed how she pictured her daughter's face most of the time she was on the air, and that when she came home her child was usually asleep. A single mother who was a feature writer told me she had to work full-time to pay the bills incurred by raising her son alone, that she wished things were different but they were what they were. My septuagenarian aunt, Gloria Liebenson, who lives in Washington and was in the audience recalled that when she adopted her second child more than thirty-five years ago she mentioned to the social worker that she was considering going back to work as an advertising executive. The social worker gave her this steely response: "You better tell me now what you're planning to do before we proceed with the adoption. This child has already lost one mother, we will not allow her to lose another one." My aunt did not go back to work in advertising, but she did start a home business in interior design to be near her kids. I felt blessed to be a writer, a profession where home and the workplace can also be one and the same.

The popular media did little to help us refrain from judging other women in the months that followed, an era in which film and television presented a plethora of conflicting messages and conflicted females. Rebecca DeMornay's portrayal of a killer nanny in *The Hand That Rocks the Cradle* shot a bolt through every working woman who had child care in the home. Cool, scrappy, and married to her job, single journalist Murphy Brown confounded us all in the last episode of the 1992 season by stepping out of character and giving birth. Roseanne showed the bold face of housewifery, but there was little display of compassion to soften her roar. Now *Thelma & Louise*, they were wild, wilder, wildest, as fearless friends who packed pistols and were unswerving in their mission to put men in their place. But they killed to get ahead. Why were they any different than the psychopath nanny who tries to murder her employer and kidnap the children in *The Hand That Rocks the Cradle*?

The signals were all over the map. What were we supposed to think? That feminism was evil? That feminism was dead? That women can never win? None of the celluloid role models that were paraded in front of us looked very appealing. I had to become my own role model. The tug of my children was winning over my desire to forge upward in my career, yet I was still living the core elements of feminist ideology—equality, power, independence, and freedom.

Equality? Chuck was my partner, even for the grimiest of chores. This is a man who clips the coupons, does the grocery shopping, is in charge of hair-washing and baths, can whip off an old Huggie and fasten a new one faster than any husband, and is as touchy and tender with his sons as any mother. All this, and he's home by 6:30 P.M.

Power? For the first time on any job I was not ac[
to anyone.

Independence? I was in charge of dozens of cri[
sions, from what my kids wore, to what they ate, to the best
places to sign them up for karate, tumbling, and art lessons.

Freedom? As a mother running an enterprise of children,
I was shattering the glass ceiling to be anyone I wanted to be.
Talk about real freedom, freedom unleashed! I had become the
unrestrained goddess in a house of males. I didn't Have It All,
but, Lord, did I have plenty.

SURRENDERING TO MARRIAGE

"If you want to reach your goal don't scatter your shots," my
father had always told me as I was spreading my efforts in a
dozen directions and complaining I wasn't getting what I
wanted or wanting what I got. What did I want now? Healthy
children and lots of them. A strong marriage. Spiritual growth.
I had to focus on this slice for now, and if that meant not having
it all, I was better off. All is nothing, a slice can be everything.
Being a mother first and a writer second was starting to feel
right, especially by that autumn, when I became pregnant again.
Chuck was appalled; I was ebullient. He who coined the motto
"Four Before Forty" couldn't fathom the idea that when the
baby was born the following spring we would have three children under the age of three. But as two sonograms showed a
healthy fetus with a tiny beating heart, my husband began to
get thrilled, too.

I was expectant and joyful to be yielding to the Higher
Power of Children in the fall of 1992. There was a baby growing
inside of me, Theo had started nursery school, and several of
the mothers of kids in his class who had also taken the steam
out of their careers to be at home became my dearest friends:
Sherry, a lawyer; Tracy, a Ph.D. in cognitive psychology; Mary

Kay, a Ph.D. candidate in education; Mariella, a public relations consultant; Amy, a journalist; and Joan, a promotional director for a supermarket chain. The way we fell together like sisters reminded us of the meshing of a fantastic dormitory floor freshman year in college. We met every morning after drop-off and lingered over coffee and gossip. We met with bag lunches at Turtle Park and sat in the sandbox with our kids. We met for dinner at someone's house for pizza when our husbands would be home late from work. We laughed and we drank wine and we talked about being reborn at thirty-one or thirty-seven or in Tracy's case, at forty-two. It was the kind of female survival circle my mother had in the 1960s with Libby, Sylvia, Ruth, Shirley, Estelle, and Eileen.

Nearly three months into body changes and mulling over names, I miscarried just before Christmas. Grief gripped me through the holidays and for the first part of the new year. I'd tell myself how lucky I was to have what I already had. My husband was loyal and steadfast. Our boys were healthy and bright. I still had my writing, and I was teaching a journalism seminar one afternoon a week at American University. But confidence in my career didn't help me shake that feeling of gloom, of mangled dreams, that somehow God knew I couldn't handle another child, that there was still career-karma to work out. Well, I'll show God, I was thinking as I marked my ovulation days on the calendar.

God showed me instead—a sonogram in March revealed two amniotic sacs, two fluttering heartbeats, two babies to be born in November 1993. TWINS! Your trouble begins when you get what you want. The radiologist confirmed that what we were seeing on the screen was indeed "healthy fraternal twins." An ashen Chuck sputtered: "This is impossible. There are no twins in my family." The doctor told him that twins were determined by the maternal gene. Then I reminded Chuck about my twin great-uncles Sam and Joe from Warsaw, those wonderful immigrants who sent for my mother's family, who had survived the Holocaust to move to the United States.

We left the radiology department of Columbia Hospital for Women not touching, not talking, each of us lost in our own heads. I don't know what my husband was thinking, but I remember as I held the black-and-white picture of our twin seven-week-old fetuses to my chest I was rushing like a river somewhere so deep, somewhere in the hair-thin capillaries of the two hearts that would become Jackson Robert and Zane Henry.

I started expanding quickly. By three months I looked as large as I did at six months when carrying Isaac and Theo. I had always loved being pregnant, that sensation of being ripe and voluptuous and horny. I loved the undulation of life within, the link with the Almighty, the divine spark you feel while carrying out the most ordinary of tasks. With twins the physical and the hormonal and the spiritual come at you with the gust of a hurricane, so basically by the middle of your gestation you can't do anything else but Be Pregnant. You are forced to stop, to Be There, the bulk of your body leavens the churnings of your mind. I had landed in true Zen. No longer a person, I Was Pure, Hot Pain.

My groin and back muscles burned every time I stood up, two heads were lodged against my bladder, four legs and four arms were crowding my lungs and my intestines. I'd never felt physical agony like this before, but I also had never felt such elation. When our babies arrived Chuck and I would be the parents of four children under the ages of three *before* we turned forty—we had surpassed our fantasy. The morning we went back to Columbia Hospital for amniocentesis, I remember walking through the lobby and throbbing in so many places I barely made it to the elevator. Chuck looked at me and said, "You gotta do it, we still have a long way to go." I had to do it and I would do it, for twins whose survival depended on me going the distance and for toddlers Theo and Isaac, who needed a vigorous mommy to hold them and take them fun places.

During the sonogram to pinpoint the right position for inserting the needle for the amniocentesis, Chuck and I saw two penises on the screen, sticking straight up—they seemed to be waving. Four boys! Oh, God. Three weeks later the sonogram results confirmed that, yes, what we were carrying were a couple of males, and that Twin A and Twin B were perfect little guys so far. After getting the good news, I hung up the phone from my longtime ob-gyn, Dr. Janet Schaffel, put my head in my hands and cried and prayed: Thank you, God, for blessing these babies. Thank you for Theo and Isaac and Chuck.

When you are huge with child, people get in your face and say all sorts of things, every pregnant woman knows this. Old women grab your arm, and tell you about their own pregnancy fifty years ago. When you're really huge like I was getting they ask you "How many are in there?" I would tell them two and then without skipping a beat strangers would drill me about what fertility drugs I had taken. I would then tell them that this incredible bulge in my belly was not the result of fertility treatments; these two babies were the result of having great sex twice one snowy day in February, at dawn and at midnight. That never failed to terminate the conversation.

My salvation during the summer and winter when my body got unwieldy and Theo and Isaac grew needier was Debbie Wolman, the mother of triplets who lived nearby. Debbie and I had been the closest of friends since she moved to Oak Park at the beginning of sixth grade. We always had a sisterly competition between us, and Debbie carried her triplets—Julie, Brian, and Danny—to thirty-six weeks. When they were born in February 1983 they each weighed close to five pounds. And if Debbie could do three, I could certainly do two.

I would call her every morning, complaining about my searing muscles. She always said the same thing: "You can do

it. Just get to thirty-two weeks, then anything after that is gravy."
When I got to thirty-two weeks, she said: "You can do it, just
get to thirty-six weeks." When I got to thirty-six weeks, she said:
"You can do it, just get to thirty-eight weeks." When I got close
to thirty-eight weeks, I begged my doctor to "take these babies
out!" Dr. Schaffel said, "You can do it. Just get to thirty-nine
weeks." I told her no, I could not do it, that I did not want to
do it, that I had done it, that it was Time!

Late in the afternoon of Monday, November 8, 1993, a half
hour after I had finished reading a profile of Sly Stallone in
Vanity Fair, Jack came into the world weighing 5 pounds 1
ounce. Three pushes and he arrived squawling, with lots of black
hair, scrawny chicken legs, and a red, round face that looked
like my mother's. In order to help Zane out, a two-hundred-
pound nurse had to squeeze me like a tube of toothpaste, while
I bore down for my life. Zane appeared eleven minutes after his
twin without a sound, with blond wisps, a wrestler's build at 6
pounds 4 ounces, and a complexion like a ghost. Seconds after
delivering Zane, I sat up on the bed and starting screaming: "Do
something, he looks sick." There was a team of six doctors and
nurses surrounding me telling me to lie back down, but he was
so white and he wasn't crying and I was sure that he wasn't
breathing as they laid him on my belly still attached to the um-
bilical cord. For nearly five minutes that felt like an eternity I
thought that one of the babies wasn't going to make it.

But when the neonatal specialist whisked away my pale and
placid Twin B to suction the gook out of his mouth and wrap
him in a blanket, Zane started to turn the robust color of Jack.
He never did give us a hearty, welcoming wail, he eased his way
into life, open-eyed and closed-mouthed. After birthing those
two boys and two placentas, a surge of bravado filled me up.
When I looked over at Chuck, who had witnessed the gory
scene, his eyes were closed and he looked like he might pass out.
I closed my eyes and faded, too. Later that evening in my hos-

pital room, I woke from a haze to this clear and wondrous image: my husband holding Jack and Zane, one in each hand, twined between fingers that were nearly as long as the children were. Precious twin newborns belonged to us, they were mine, Chuck was mine, Theo and Isaac were mine, I was set.

But rather than enter the happily-ever-after Rest of Our Lives stage we plotted out with ardor, we would begin a tortuous road riddled with land mines. November 8, 1993, a day surging with new life, was also the day Chuck found out his father had been hospitalized, the beginning of the end for Charles E. Anthony, Jr., who had been diagnosed with cirrhosis of the liver. So instead of being able to bask in our new babies in twin bassinets at the very beginning of their life cycles, Chuck spent the first three months of Jack and Zane's life at his father's bedside watching him die. His demise was brutal and quick. Too sick to be considered a candidate for a transplant, my father-in-law died on his sixty-fifth birthday.

Chuck fell into a brooding silence—remote and removed and untouchable. He had just started to get close to his dad after an estrangement that went back to his childhood. Charles E. Anthony, Jr., a Korean War hero and old-school male, boasted about Chuck to his friends but showed little outward affection toward his boy. Throughout his father's horrific illness, I never saw Chuck cry. He simply got quieter and thinner and more distant.

The births that coincided with death marked the darkest period of our marriage. All of our own unresolved issues came to a blistering head. My friends were raving about author John Gray's *Men Are from Mars, Women Are from Venus.* But I couldn't bring myself anywhere near this book that promises on its cover to improve communication so you can get what you want from your relationship. I knew enough about the sharp differences between men and women without anyone spelling them out for me.

I hired a baby nurse from Baltimore with one-and-a-half-inch fingernails decorated with flower decals to help with the twins. Bernice had moved back to North Carolina to be near her family, and we hired a nanny to help with the older boys. Having a nurse and a nanny was more money than we should have spent at a juncture in our marriage when Chuck's architectural practice was practically at a halt. But the company of other capable women to help with four children under the age of three was necessary for my mental health at a time when my partner in parenting was often not around. I tried to concentrate on giving my all to make Theo and Isaac feel secure in the new pecking order, but giving my all at that time was not very much.

The Supermama who could have shouted "Free at last!" from rooftops was listless. My psyche was flat and empty as my abdomen minus the twins. My energy was sucked dry by two insatiable little breastfeeders. My heart was split among four children who each needed more than they were getting. I turned to Antoine in Jean-Paul Sartre's *Nausea* to speak to my own anguish, he who describes his state as being "illuminated within by a diminishing light." That line reminded me of my own dwindling internal candle, the charred chunk of dwarfed wax that not long ago had been an incandescent pillar. As I read *Nausea* on a rainy April afternoon in bed, the sky was charcoal and the trees were rustling in the cold wind. Theo and Isaac were squealing with laughter downstairs in the living room, but I remained separate, sulking in my cave, receiving nothing, giving nothing, drowning like Antoine in a nausea I couldn't shake.

Jack and Zane were nursing, and I was about to start sobbing when Theo and Isaac came bounding up the stairs, hurling their little bodies upon my legs. Instantly, they blew apart my blues and self-absorption. God, how I wished Chuck could be here, too, to be part of this pile of love that was ours. God, how I wished Chuck was still smitten like he was that night at the Lebanese Taverna when I was talking to him about God and he gave me his red-and-green sweater to put on and it felt like I was crawling into his skin. What happened to my fantasy of marriage as a melding of souls? Where was Chuck? He was mourning in his mother's living room sixty miles away.

I needed my husband, and what my husband needed the most right then was for me not to be needy, to leave him the hell alone. In between birth and death and the emotional upheaval that comes with both, we bought an old house on a river near the Chesapeake Bay that required lots of work. Chuck signed on as general contractor and architect, an enormous task that meant blending part of a one-hundred-year-old shingled house with an addition that looked like it had come with the original structure. Because of no-show carpenters, masons, and drywall crews, Chuck, and a couple of his high school buddies, ended up building most of the house themselves.

The finished product is extraordinary, with crannies and rich woodwork reminiscent of the Frank Lloyd Wright houses in my hometown of Oak Park and the craftsman cottages of Southern California. But the toll it took on Chuck, already reeling from losing his father, was also extraordinary. This house devoured him, a project where old walls and old floors he had nearly finished fixing would suddenly crumble, and he'd have to start again from scratch. Anyone who has ever renovated an old house had warned me that the process could destroy a marriage. I heard over and over how a job as small as enlarging a bathroom could throw you into psychotherapy. When we moved from Washington to the country on January 23, 1995, our marriage did indeed nearly come crumbling down, strewn among the heaps of plaster and rotted-out debris with rusty nails in our Dumpster. We were drained by four of life's top stress-inducers: birth, death, moving, and construction.

It was effortless to surrender to my children in the house on the river with the red-tile Mexican floor that felt wonderful to walk across barefoot in the morning. But to Chuck Anthony, the man who had given me my dreams, I wasn't surrendering at all. Did I have to give in to marriage, too? It was only when Chuck and I had finally pushed each other to the perilous precipice, and we were dangling there staring into the abyss, that the answer to that question became clear—almost too late.

Three weeks after we moved into our house with its cedar shingles and magnificent sunlight spilling in, my husband of nearly seven years jammed boxer shorts, corduroy trousers, a striped sweater I had given him for his thirty-fifth birthday, and his leather toilet kit into his black canvas bag and said he was moving out. While he packed, he was huffing about how he was never coming back, how this was absolutely, definitely The End.

Throughout our marriage there had been other threats, but then dawn came and sleepy embraces and we ended up together at the breakfast table laughing with the amazing children we made. And I would be thinking: no one will ever help me care for these kids like their father will. No one will know that Theo can't sleep unless his white Power Ranger doll is on his pillow, that Isaac can't sleep without his monkey puppet, that Jack and Zane can't sleep without their yellow blankets folded by their heads. What new man would want to walk into this life? And even if Chuck did leave he would never really be gone because there would be four little boys in my house who look like him. But this explosion was different: This "four before forty" achieved in less than four years had frayed us to our breaking point. And so there I was, on an idyllic hill flanked by children, looking out my kitchen window at river, as the man who made my fairy tale come true was adding on an unhappy ending.

I should have seen this moment coming long before we stood beneath the chuppa at the Standard Club in March 1988. How could I have believed that Charles E. Anthony III, whose family came to America from England in the late 1600s, could connect in an abiding way with Iris Bessie Krasnow, whose Polish mother landed at Ellis Island in 1952. We are opposites in every way. He is guarded; I am revelatory. He hates mornings; I shoot out of bed at 5:45 A.M. ready for anything. Chuck thinks my family is too direct; I think his family is too indirect. Figuring out buildings is his primary fascination; I yearn to figure out people. He isn't sure he believes in God; my God is everything. Our only common trait is that we both hate green peppers.

Yet, scarred and scared by the loss of my father, this is the solid and comforting man I married. Drawn to a shared vision of domesticity and forever, we walked down the aisle to the Beatles' song "Here, There and Everywhere," and read these lines from the Book of Ruth during the ceremony: "Where you go I will go, and where you stay I will stay. Your people will be my people and your God my God. Where you die I will die, and there I will be buried. May the Lord deal with me, be it ever so severely, if anything but death separates you and me."

A month after our wedding I was pregnant. Then came a miscarriage. Then came Theo. Then came Isaac. Then came a miscarriage. Then came Jack and Zane. Boggled by five pregnancies and four babies and six years of no sleep, we never had the chance to nurture and baby each other. He was asleep when I rose at 5:30 A.M. to fetch squawling infants, and immersed in architecture books when I collapsed into bed at 9 P.M.

We had no leisure time to talk about our days, our prized old Scrabble board hadn't been out of its box since our first anniversary in St. Barts. Had he wanted to get close to me, it would have been impossible; I was always covered with bodies. When we did exchange conversation it was to divvy up assignments—who would take the twins to the pediatrician for HIB shots, who would buy Huggies on sale at the Safeway, who would handle the twins' night feeding. My solace from a marriage that made me feel alone more than adored was the glorious pack of boys that smothered me with juicy kisses. I was, unquestionably, the revered queen of the house. But the king was defecting.

When the day came in February that he closed the front door carrying his bag and left me with a twin on each hip, I felt oddly euphoric at first, strange as that may seem. To be through with Chuck, the hard, silent man I loved but didn't want to be around, would be emancipating. Then I could infuse my sons with the qualities I wished all males had, such as tenderness and the gift of gab, undeterred by a macho mate. I was already picturing my next husband, someone short, urgent, and communicative. The euphoria quickly dissipated during a day spent chasing boys and trying to keep them smiling when my foundation was in smithereens.

There is no way to prepare yourself for the meltdown of a marriage and the liquid pain that swirls through your body, through every space where you walk. It zaps you in the bedroom where his blue terrycloth bathrobe lies like a dead body on the Berber carpet of jewel tones you picked together when you were about to start over in a new riverfront house. It hits you in the bathroom that smells of his Mennen Speedstick and where his boxers with candy canes are strewn near the shower. It's a pain that feels like a bullet tearing into your flesh as you have to listen to two one-year-olds say "Bye-bye Daddy's car" over and over as their faces are pressed against the kitchen window staring at the empty driveway in front of the house where a Red Nissan truck is usually parked.

Oh, God, now what? Please help me muster up the strength to pretend that all is merry so my boys don't have even a teensy little clue that their lives are in the Cuisinart. And so with a false smile on my face and a knife in my soul I pretended to carry on, putting Jack and Zane down for their naps, sticking Theo and Isaac in front of *Home Alone.* Then I buried my face in our flannel comforter and cried into a feather pillow that smelled like Chuck. I cried and cried until the pain was out, and tender scenes of our courtship washed over me.

I thought about the time when Chuck led me by the hand

as if I were a child onto the plane that would take me to my father's deathbed, telling the stewardess to take care of me, then whispering "I love you" and kissing my forehead. I thought about the gift I brought back to Chuck as a thank-you for taking care of Max the cat and watering my plants while I was gone for a month—a small print of an African mother sitting in a field with her baby tied up in a big scarf on her back. Browsing through a crafts shop in Coronado, California, I was certain when I stopped in front of that woman with child that it was right for this Chuck I had only known two months. It was a profound knowing that had nothing to do with my brain. I thought of the gift Chuck had bought me years later at an art fair in Tucson, Arizona, after my first miscarriage when I was sure I'd never have any children—a silver fertility goddess neck-lace.

I thought about something else he would often say as I carried on about how we weren't meant to be, how we weren't meshed in spirit like you must be in marriage. He'd say in that soft voice that you had to crane to hear that we were part of a destiny that we could no longer change or rearrange. That by making first one boy, then two, then three, then four, we were soulmates in the largest sense even if we didn't think we were or didn't want to be. I'd press him: "Well, how do you know we should stay together?" And he'd stare at me with those eyes that always made me feel bathed in light: "Because you are my wife."

According to Thomas Moore, author of *Soul Mates: Honoring the Mysteries of Love and Relationship*, having faith in that "fateful spirit" that brings people together in the first place could be just the Letting Go that I needed.

As Moore writes: "From the viewpoint of soul, nothing happens by accident. The fatefulness that surrounds the beginning of a profound relationship suggests an intentionality far beyond the ken of the people involved. In acknowledging this turn of fate, we may find some peace and grounding, and also some humility as the relationship continues to offer unexpected challenges. Throughout the relationship we could remember its fateful beginnings, and notice further signals that the marriage has an impetus from beyond the couple's intentions."

That impetus from beyond, the spirit that pushes you forward no matter how much the mind has convinced you to stop, was apparent each time I looked at one of our kids and saw pieces of Chuck, pieces of me, a composite of our beings. Theo and Isaac and Jack and Zane with their spindly bodies and wild hair and blue-green eyes are what we did together, and from that fact there was no escape, karma had brought us irrevocably to this place. In other words, in the Now, with Four Under Four, we were stuck. And although we could often not stand each other on a day-to-day basis, we owed it to all of us to figure out a way to spend a lifetime together. This was no simple chore.

As a woman who had a prolonged single life, I was a stranger to belonging to one person and staying in one place. So I wasn't swooning, like Mrs. Norman Vincent Peale was in *The Adventures of Being a Wife,* about being "one integrated, mutually responsive, mutually supportive organism" with her Norman. Nor did I share the Oneness of many of my friends' marriages. With their only daughter grown and out of the house, Amber drinks brandy at midnight with her husband, Eric, at an antique roundtable for two in their bedroom. Siobhan calls Steven "sweetie" when she talks to him on the phone. My sister and Seth seem to be always holding hands. "We're so close you couldn't stick a knife blade between us," Mrs. Peale gushes of her Norman.

And here I was, often feeling as if you could stick an entire ocean between me and Chuck. Who was this man? I did not know. He was as foreign to my constitution as the Iron Man of Robert Bly. Yet when he returned home ten hours after leaving that Saturday in February, at 9:07 A.M., I jumped into his arms.

That night, as we lay in bed on opposite sides, he told me all the awful things about me and I told him all the despicable things about him. We were back in the quicksand. I asked him if he felt even a shard of hope that we could make it.

After a few minutes Chuck grumbled, "Well, maybe a shard."

We decided to get into therapy immediately. Staring into the abyss, we either had to be coached out of jumping or cushioned for the fall. After getting the names of the three leading marriage counselors in town I found myself talking on my car phone to an Israeli-born psychotherapist named Ruth. I told her that my husband and I were on the brink of splitting, then I gave her a one-minute snapshot of personal history, the improbability of our marriage, the four boys under four, how I was wired and he was tired, the ocean between us. She laughed, I couldn't believe it, then said she was perfect for us: "Counseling couples on the brink is what I do best."

During some sessions Chuck and I believe in the spiritual rightness of our union, during others we sit on opposite ends of Ruth's couch done up in soothing, sweeping mauve spitting out venomous accusations. On those bleakest of days, she always says the same thing: "You've got to work this out." And so we work and I cry and Chuck retreats and we fight and we see Ruth and I get fearful that we lack the grit to make our marriage endure. But then I'm sitting with the four boys at our kitchen table and I am hypnotized by their faces that are ancient mosaics of Krasnows and Anthonys, and then I'm walking through Barnes & Noble and finding myself at the cash register spending $19.95 for Hugh and Gayle Prather's book *I Will Never Leave You: How Couples Can Achieve the Power of Lasting Love.*

If the Prathers can make it, anyone can. Hugh, the author of the 1970s bible *Notes to Myself*, had affairs for half their thirty-plus-year marriage. Now in the business of counseling couples, the Prathers deliver plenty of insightful prose on the pages of *I Will Never Leave You*, a book with this bottom line: You, too, Can Live Happily Ever After with Your Mate, No Matter How Big of a Shmuck He or She Has Been.

As they write: "The enormous spiritual cost of betrayal and abandonment is presently being so miscalculated that an entire generation is in danger of becoming emotionally and spiritually bankrupt . . . we can tell you unequivocally that after more than two decades of helping couples with their marriages and almost three decades of working on our own, we have rarely encountered anyone whose life was made happier by the act of abandoning his or her partner."

When mothers I meet find out we have four sons under the age of five, the next question always is: How do you do it? I tell them without trepidation that we enlist the services of a good marriage therapist. Many people become embarrassed, as if I've just admitted to being nuts. My feeling is this: Going for counseling is not a sign of emotional weakness. Counseling requires emotional heroism. It takes a groundswell of courage to get out of the finger-pointing mode and to look within for change and growth. It takes a brave person to make your marriage work.

Further incentive to improve the quality of your relationship can come from studying divorced friends around you. Debbie Wolman, the angel who pushed me through my twin pregnancy, wed right out of college, had a difficult time conceiving, went for fertility treatment, and got three babies. She and her husband divorced when the children were nearly five. That sweltering August night I wore a floral polyester bridesmaid gown at her wedding played back vividly as Debbie uttered these unforgettable words when her spouse moved out of the house: "I know there are going to be problems in any relationship. I think I should have tried harder to work out those problems with the father of my children."

In the several years since Debbie's divorce, she has had assorted serious relationships with very different men. I've watched closely; it's been a real education on what's Out There and it's made Chuck look very stable and desirable. One was a forty-six-year-old divorced father of two teenagers who restored vintage cars and used to pick Debbie up for their dates on a Harley. Next came the twenty-eight-year-old tennis pro at a country club who was a ringer for Tony Danza and spent money he didn't have. Debbie's lot as a single parent living with three adolescents is a far different family than what she had growing up. "Iris, you and I lived in a house where our parents stayed together until death did they part," she says.

Until death did they part, indeed. Debbie's mother, Ellen Glasser, died of breast cancer at age fifty-nine after being married to her husband, Marvin, for thirty-seven years. When my father died at sixty-seven, my parents were about to celebrate their thirty-fifth anniversary. I was thirty-one, my sister was thirty-two, my brother was twenty-nine. We were the adult children of a mother and father who fought, loved each other, and stayed married. Knowing nothing else but an unbroken time line linking all your memories from birth makes you want to re-create that continuity for yourself. It's not always possible, of course, but if that "shard of love" is there, there is potential to go the distance with the partner with whom you vowed you would do just that.

Surrendering to the spiritual force that made you fall in love in the first place even when it feels like that force is leaking through a colander is a giant leap of faith—but it is necessary. I know this to be true even though I sometimes fight The Force with clenched fists and a hardened heart. Surrender to Him? Oh, God, did I have to do that, too? To resign myself to the fact that Chuck and I are It? To do what I said I'd do when we became husband and wife? I knew in other arenas of life that if you stick by your commitments, your life works to its maximum efficiency. This was the best lesson from the est training: "Do what you say you're going to do." If you stay committed to a marriage the payoff is that you can eventually attain a state of divine enlightenment, where you see that it was meant to be after all:

"Most couples can look back in old age and see a rightness, almost a perfection, to all they went through together," write the Prathers in *I Will Never Leave You.*

"The strengths that one partner has almost invariably complement the other's weaknesses. This coincidence is so striking that it seems mystical. And perhaps it is. . . . It's as if God sent you the box of your missing parts."

Chuck argues today that during those months I felt unloved and abandoned he was actually loving me completely, by designing and doing much of the building of a new home for our burgeoning family. The Caveman was bringing me shelter, in his perception the supreme act of caring. Women want verbal reinforcement; guys often think that drywalling a kitchen and chainsawing the hedges is proof enough of their affections. And I married a Guy, the sort who likes cigars and football and work boots.

This I do know: If this man does pack up his black canvas bag again and we do move on to new relationships, we will bring the problems we never resolved to our next partners, as my friend Debbie realized when her marriage was over. Or even worse, we will miss the spouse we left behind. I did, after all, marry this man one snowy March night holding red roses and white orchids and visions of lots of babies. After we were pronounced husband and wife, the pianist played the Beatles' song of enduring love, "When I'm Sixty-Four."

I knew it wouldn't be easy. As a person hooked on change and pushing through today to get to something better, living with someone, steadily, for the long haul, would be a lifelong struggle, perhaps it's the ultimate struggle for a generation that has had a taste of everything. Coming off conquest after conquest, it's a slap to realize that where you are now just may be your landing spot. That this Is It! Sometimes I feel as outraged by that prospect as I did when I first read the Oriana Fallaci essay "Why I Never Married" that appeared in the December 1974 *Ms.* magazine. As a twenty-year-old college student with the wind at my back, author-activist Fallaci summed up my sentiments of the season in this paragraph: "The profession of wife has always filled me with horror. I did not want to play the wife. I wanted to write, to travel, to know the world, to use the miracle of having been born. And, as if this weren't enough, I couldn't stand the idea of giving up my name to take the name of a man. To give it up, why? To annul myself like that, why? I was mine."

With four rollicky boys in my charge, I read through Fallaci's essay again. My reaction was that I may have been mine once, but I am the children's now. This outpouring of Self into my sons came naturally in a way I did not have to ponder and could not control. What I needed to figure out was how the I that is mine could give the Him that is Chuck the piece of me he wanted and complained he wasn't getting.

During my interviews for United Press International with strong-minded women who seemed to be good at being wives, I always sought answers on ways to stick with one man. How do you make your marriage succeed? It was my favorite question to pose to subjects ranging from Yoko Ono to Barbara Bush to Queen Noor of Jordan. Reading those interviews years later, when I needed all the advice I could get, I found plenty of inspiration.

Smoke from a chain of Camels swirled around Yoko as she sat cross-legged in a plush white chair in her white office. She was dressed in one of Lennon's Hawaiian shirts that billowed around her diminutive frame, and a heart-shaped diamond, a gift from her late husband, dangled at her throat. Yoko spoke at length about "what happened," as she recalled the black night when her forty-year-old husband was murdered, often gazing at the huge portrait of Lennon and a young Sean a couple of feet away. The father and son who share the same birthday, October 9, both had shoulder-length hair in the painting.

When I met Yoko Ono for this interview in June 1984, she was fifty-one years old. She agreed to this session because she was preparing to auction off memorabilia of her life with Lennon at Sotheby's, and she wanted the "family of the world" to know about this event, which was to benefit the Spirit Foundation, an organization created by Yoko and Lennon to help fund children's causes. For Yoko to enter the century-old Dakota apartment on Central Park West meant having to walk where she was walking with John Lennon the night he was shot. Yet she had stoically chosen to continue living there, "surrounded by the things John and I loved," as she told me.

I asked her if she felt that in a person's life there is only one great love.

"Well, you see it's hard for me to get off this sort of train that I'm on, which is John's and my life. Only because it was cut off in the middle," she said, puffing hard on a Camel.

"If we had gone through the whole phase of being together and it was like, logically, we were going to separate, then it would have been different. But it was right at the moment when we were excited about the future and all that. So it's hard. And I didn't know that it would take this long, but it just takes a whole lot to sort out the emotions. John and I had such an intense relationship. When we met, we knew that we knew. Maybe now I feel like I need a rest from that kind of intense relationship. I can't imagine having another one like that."

John Lennon had devoted the first years of their son Sean's life to being the primary parent at home, while Yoko Ono ran their business ventures. Their much wanted son came as a hard-earned gift after a string of miscarriages. Having optimum time and attention from parents who cherished him in turn made Sean a doting and attentive son. (When last heard from, the twenty-year-old Sean was touring the country and yelping and whooping with his sixty-two-year-old mother in their rock trio called IMA. In the March 18, 1996, issue of *Newsweek* he admiringly described the tenor of the group: "We're just doing the Yoko thing. It's totally, full-on Yoko." A decade earlier I had asked Sean's unconquerable mother if she thought she and John set an example of a new equality in marriage.

"I think it's definitely a very practical way for a modern couple to live," she told me. "Because the stress of society is so great, a man needs an equally strong woman and a woman needs a strong man as a partner. It's also good to have two people coming from totally different backgrounds with different opinions and ideas to join together.

"That way, that particular unit will have a very wide range of understanding and power together. I mean, the richness of our unity—there are things that John covered that I couldn't cover or I covered and John couldn't cover."

The richness of their unity—Yoko Ono's description of the yin-yang of her marriage was heartening. It was a noble goal in matrimony; to aspire toward being concentric circles not rotating orbs in separate spheres. I told her that I had read that she had once said "by connecting with John, I became anchored." Did she still feel anchored, in spite of everything?

"Yes," she said immediately. "And I think the reverse works, too. Now that he's out there, the spirit, by connecting with his root, which is us, he's probably anchored and will live forever with us."

As Chuck and I sat in the family room just before Thanksgiving 1995 watching the Beatles' reunion television special, I saw a young, cool Yoko in a micromini with long black hair, the avant-garde performance artist who met a Beatle in 1966 and shook up rock and roll history. I remembered her telling me that John had provided her with an anchor.

Four months before his death, Lennon told *Playboy* magazine that when he wrote the words for "Lucy in the Sky with Diamonds," he was conceptualizing "the image of the female who would someday come save me—a 'girl with kaleidoscope eyes.' It turned out to be Yoko, though I hadn't met Yoko yet."

I was reminded of what my kids' preschool director Ellie Martin had told me about children, that all they really want to know is that there is someone there to take care of them, someone to save them from themselves. The same holds true for grownups, especially those who lived the illusions and weirdness of the sixties and seventies.

What Chuck Anthony had brought to me was also an anchor, having roped me in from some turbulent waters. Sitting on our family-room couch, four children down for the night, we listened to the Beatles music that had been around since we were in bell-bottoms and kissing for the first time in junior high, when all of life lay open to us. And this is where we had arrived—married, on a couch stained with purple Juicy Juice, watching television, in robes and slippers.

As much as we believed our generation would be far out forever, perennial trippers on a Yellow Submarine, we were turning out to be as square as our parents in their station wagons. The times only seemed to be a-changing with psychedelics and cosmic relationships, but the heart of man and woman remains ruled by a primal desire to be anchored in a family—even if the trade-off means a loss of breathless anticipation and open-ended dreams. For me, trying to change the world and trying to change the Self had given way to a stronger urge—trying to find the soul. Of all the places I've been and people I've been, I found that divine cave as a homebody.

From nearly the moment she laid eyes on him as a teenager,

Barbara Bush never wanted anything more than to make a home with the man she loved. She was a sixteen-year-old student from a South Carolina prep school when George Herbert Walker Bush came up to her at a Christmas dance in his hometown of Greenwich, Connecticut. He was seventeen, a senior at Phillips Academy, and navy bound. She dropped out of Smith College at the age of nineteen to marry Bush, then a Yale man, in 1945. When I interviewed Barbara Bush over tea in the vice-president's mansion, she was on the last lap of her husband's 1988 presidential campaign, during which she had come forth proudly as a "housewife" who doesn't meddle in the business of her spouse. She had been too absorbed in being the force that bound a family of five children whose father was often gone, first building oil businesses, then serving as a congressman and a United Nations ambassador, leading the Republican National Committee, heading the CIA, and being the vice president of the United States.

She shook her head in a hearty no when asked if she felt that her own aspirations were throttled along the way.

"I didn't like to study very much," said Mrs. Bush. "I was all right in high school, but when it came to Smith, I was a cliffhanger. The truth is, I just wasn't very interested. I was just interested in George.

"I'm not sorry I didn't go back to college. If I wanted to I would have. I could have done anything I wanted. But I wouldn't change a day of my life."

She recalled with an adolescent's grin that at the beginning, "our relationship was breathless." I asked her how to make breathlessness turn into a marriage that lasts for forty-three years. Her advice was to first "pick a good husband." And tell the truth.

"I'm also coming to the conclusion, having talked to people forever—you go through great self-analysis when you're running for president, I feel like I'm on a couch all the time—

that maybe it's thinking not about what I feel, but 'What is he feeling? Am I answering his needs?' And utmost honesty is very important. You ought to say to your husband sometimes, 'You know, I gotta tell you the honest truth. That hurt my feelings.' "

The public may not have picked up on the lighter side of George Bush, yet his wife said his humor was one quality that made an "enormous difference" in the trying stretches of their long marriage. "I'm thinking about the most awful day of my life, after our daughter Robin died," at age three of leukemia in 1953. "I'd been so strong all that time, and George had been so hurt by this beautiful creature dying that he could barely be with her. . . . I just fell apart when she died. I said, 'George, I just can't go downstairs.' There were all those people down there" in their house.

"He looked out the window and saw my darling sister, Martha Rafferty, coming up the driveway with her husband. And he said, 'Here are the O'Raffertys. It's going to be a hell of a wake.' And somehow or other, it made it better. It was so sweet, that I was all right. If it wasn't for that, I would not have gotten down those damned stairs." This grandmother of eleven with the pure-white hair grabbed a Kleenex as tears streamed down her cheeks etched with deep lines. She shrugged her shoulders and looked at me with a profound sadness that she had not shaken in the thirty-five years since her toddler daughter died. I had yet to become a parent, but I knew then that when you lose a child you can never be totally happy again.

George Bush was not one of my favorite politicians, but I liked him more after hearing about his personal side. What I understood from that anecdote describing their daughter's wake was that he was sensitive to the needs of his wife. And what she needed in the pit of grief over death was to be reminded of the life and love that remained, in the form of her sister coming toward her house, in a husband doing his best to cheer her up.

A few years later Mrs. Bush was asked to address Wellesley College as a graduation speaker, and there was an outcry among the student body. Here was a school that could recruit any high-voltage woman in the country to deliver a commencement speech; why settle for someone whose profession had been merely as a mother and wife? "Barbara Bush has gained recognition through the achievements of her husband," was the central protest of the Wellesley women, who stressed that their college "teaches us that we will be rewarded on the basis of our own merit, not on that of a spouse."

As a twenty-one-year-old college senior poised to topple the Old Male Guard, I, too, would have tried to get Barbara Bush recalled from an appearance at my graduation. But as a mother in my mid-thirties trying to make my marriage succeed, I was eager to listen to the politician's wife who had put family and husband before herself. Another First Lady I met, Queen Noor of Jordan, also talked about maintaining a marriage and a house full of children by gracefully accepting a backseat role.

Before Lisa Halaby became Queen Noor of Jordan, she was a student at Princeton enrolled in the university's first coed class, and one of the first women students to major in architecture and urban planning. She lived in a group house on a farm off-campus and participated in Vietnam War protests. In 1978, at the age of twenty-six, the self-described "unconventional" young woman who ripened during the peak of the pacifist and feminist movements became a Sunni Muslim and married King Hussein, forty-two, monarch of Jordan, a war-torn, patriarchal place. We all watched as the ambitious and adventurous Halaby turned into the elegant Queen Noor al Hussein, unwavering in her mission to stand by her man, a survivor of eleven assassination attempts, cancer, heart surgery, and being the point man in the never-ending Mideast peace process.

Halaby could have carved out a cushier, safer deal for herself. She could have settled among her wealthy Arab-American family rooted in Washington, D.C., designed houses for a career, and met friends for dinner at outdoor cafes in DuPont Circle. Instead, she lives on the other side of the globe encased in an armored palace on grounds she cannot leave without a chauffeur and security guards. While other wives think of traffic jams when their spouses are late, Queen Noor worries about bullets if the king fails to show up at a designated time.

Getting to be a queen in a fancy palace is supposed to be the grist of fairy tales. For Noor al Hussein, or the "light of Hussein," it's been one knock, one shock, after another. But the beautiful and smart Noor who could have been anything she wanted to be has chosen to help rule an Arab people who have often been harshly critical of their American queen.

For what?

"I wanted my destiny to be extraordinary . . . ," she said. "I never wanted to be like everybody else. In fact, I wanted not to be like everybody else and find my own way." In the dining room fifteen yards away, King Hussein was meeting to heal a rift with Palestine Liberation Organization leader Yasir Arafat, triggered by the PLO hijacking of the *Achille Lauro* cruise ship that resulted in the murder of Leon Klinghoffer, a New Jersey man in a wheelchair.

The queen would often stop the conversation taking place in the late autumn of 1985 to focus on Prince Hamzah, five, who was walking across the canvas sofa in his tennis shoes and on Prince Hashem, four, tearing across the Persian carpet, just missing a three-foot-high brass urn as he reached for a chocolate from a silver tray. Their one-year-old sister, Princess Iman, toddled into the room in pink slippers with mouse faces, grabbing a fistful of almonds and plopping on top of "Mummy."

I wanted my own babies so badly as I watched this woman, five months pregnant with her fourth child, and her tawny-skinned, almond-eyed brood. Although she was the first queen in the history of the Hashemite kingdom to have her own office, and had emerged as her country's unofficial ambassador speaking out on Arab-American relations, I realized the depth of her surrender to marriage, the sacrifice that was necessary to get this whole, resplendent package. Queen Noor had adapted what she called a "subservient" role to a man who ascended the throne in 1951 at age seventeen, succeeding his grandfather, King Abdullah, who was assassinated in young Hussein's presence, and who brought with him seven other children from three previous marriages.

"I believe in his work, and I believe it is even more important than me," she said of living with the world's longest-ruling monarch. "Our relationship is important as it contributes to that work; it's essentially bound up with it, and subservient to it—it has to be."

The afternoon sun cast a glow on the queen's finely chiseled face. Her golden hair was pouffed and brushed back, revealing mosaic earrings of onyx, pearl, and pea-sized rubies. On her left wrist a chain of diamonds fell over a diamond-studded gold watch, and a thick band of pavé diamonds encircled her ring finger. Beneath these lustrous relics of royalty lay a darker reality. Surrounding Nadwa Palace, where a child's green go-cart and red minibike were parked in front, were dozens of guards in fatigues and berets with submachine guns at their sides. Queen Noor complained that she would love to open her windows and get some fresh air but she couldn't because of the bullet-proof glass.

Jordan was tranquil at that time, but the Mideast conflict is "something we live and breathe all day—we are never away from it," said the queen of a country encircled by combative neighbors—Iraq, Syria, Israel, and, by extension, Lebanon. She said that King Hussein doesn't leave the house without a gun under his belt.

"He happens to be an excellent shot, so there is no point

in his not carrying one. If you are as good or better a shot than your security guards, you might as well carry your own."

Living under oppressive security with a man who is betrothed to his work still didn't make her feel trapped. Rather, she spoke of her role as the wife of King Hussein as "the pieces of my life coming together beautifully. It was like being offered the perfect job." A primary task she set out for herself is to use her Arab-American perspective as a bridge between the two cultures through educational programs and lectures in Jordan and the United States. But her biggest job is to keep the king happy, while she keeps her own "heavy burden" to herself.

"I have to be a positive force for him. I can't walk around like this." She made a glum face. "I have to be someone who can help to neutralize the effects of the pressure. That's a challenge for anyone—that's an art. And I'm sure that, God willing, I'll learn it better and better, the art of being able to neutralize the effects of pressure so I can create an atmosphere where we can live and function as healthy, balanced, normal people to as great an extent as possible.

"My husband has become my best friend over time. For us, we need each other to be that because there is nobody else we can trust."

Ten years later, I saw the queen of Jordan on television standing next to her husband at the funeral of Prime Minister Yitzhak Rabin, the king's closest compatriot in the Mideast peace process. Hussein was in tears, she seemed to be holding him up with her erect and tall body, still standing by her man after all the terrorist acts and his health scares and the enormity of the needs of the Hashemite kingdom of Jordan that will always take precedence over her. This was how things had panned out for a sharp American woman who was part of a youth culture trained first to ask "But what about me?" Her destiny had indeed turned out to be extraordinary, just as she had wanted it to be as a young activist at Princeton.

To me, the most extraordinary aspect of Queen Noor was that she had remained on board a royal life that, she said with a sarcastic laugh, "bears no resemblance to a fairy-tale existence." By marrying a king and moving to his palace, she had a great vantage point and lots of jewelry and invitations to the best parties in the world. But her destiny, however regal, wasn't about her, it was about her husband and his land.

I knew I could never give up everything that Queen Noor had given up, but I understood why she did it as I sat next to Chuck at our kitchen table watching Rabin's funeral, with kids screeching around us. For all I had accomplished as a single woman fanning a Brilliant Career, I still had been left without anything substantial to really hold on to during those years consumed by my job. Queen Noor had so much filling her heart. It was apparent when she stroked those children, and laughed lovingly as she told me that the king always sneaks them sweets when she is not looking. Quite simply, the only way she could have what she had was to discard desires of Self. I thought of my father chiding me when I sneered that getting married and having children would ruin my career: "So what's wrong with that?"

I told Chuck I couldn't believe that the Husseins had made it through seventeen years of harsh politics and Mideast bloodshed and raising all those kids.

His instant response was: "Why shouldn't they make it? They are married."

"What do you mean 'they are married'?" I asked him.

"What I mean, Iris, is that they have no other choice but to make it work. They run a country together. They have children together. Why would they want to start over?"

"But what about Charles and Diana?" I demanded to know.

"They blew it," said Chuck.

"What about our marriage?"

"Our marriage can be anything we want it to be."

"But do you feel like we belong together?" I asked.

Chuck shook his head: "Maybe you need to stop analyzing our relationship, and just have it."

I Bow to Thee

Stop thinking and just be—I had much to learn about surrendering to marriage from the surrender taking place in my living room. A pure state of being apart from the thrashings of the mind was beginning to happen big time with Theo, Isaac, Jack, and Zane. Mothering these boys, our supersonic litter, I was locked into a second-by-second relationship that Simply Was, without me having to pour any cerebral energy into it. In fact, this transition into Being There Totally came as my mental acuity was dwindling. Yielding to the needs of four small sons was giving me what Buddhism and Kierkegaard and spiked butterscotch brownies and the Nautilus curling machine couldn't— Magic in the Moment, peace with What Is, the gift of Being.

Surrender came in a blast similiar to the eruption of spirit at the Watergate Hotel when I tried to reach the Lord. It was the Oneness with the Universe I got in the High Sierras with Tim Hansel when I jumped down a rock face secured by rappelling ropes. It was the lightning-bolt awakening I experienced at the end of the est training twenty years earlier at the Jack Tarr Hotel in San Francisco. It was the rush of Ram Dass.

But rather than peak, fizzle, and die like the rest of my Ah Ha's, this burst of clarity that came from Being Where You Are When You Are There keeps getting larger and more intricate, coloring all of life in indelible hues of grass and sun and mud and trees and Legos and God. Having small kids is like the last day of summer vacation, when you are savoring every second coming at you, when you merge with that wonderful, intense, central part of Being, the sun on your face, the sand at your feet.

My children finally forced me to stop, to be present in the present, and to be happy at that destination. Here's how it happened.

It was Labor Day 1994, and a new nanny had just quit after two months. Too many hours, too many kids, more than what she had expected, more than any one nanny could do. She told me I left her alone too often to fend for four children. Bernice used to tell me I was around too much—"I can handle these babies, Iris," she'd say, shooing me out of her way. But this new one, twenty-one and just out of college, got winded right away, and I understood how she felt. I was winded, too, and bowled over by the prospect of being a Great Mother to each of my four children, a decent spouse, and a Developing Self all at once.

The nanny had accompanied us on our annual August vacation to Bethany Beach, Delaware. Every morning I would go for long walks along the Atlantic Ocean trying to sort it all out. When I came back refreshed from exercise and solitude our nanny would be knee-deep in sweaty, loud, Anthony siblings. I would hear her at night crying to her boyfriend on the telephone. She left right after we got back to Washington, and as her car door slammed I sat dumbfounded on the floor, where Jack and Zane and Isaac were having crawling races, each wearing only a bulging diaper. Theo was still in his X-men pajamas enraptured by Big Bird's Christmas video.

So this was it; everything I had ever wanted and strived hard to get was now mine, a husband, a nest to fluff, a batch of children, as many as Queen Noor. I had the most kids of any of our friends. But swatches of who I used to be and who I was now bombarded me as I got off the floor, changed three Huggies on the brink of exploding, and went to the kitchen to scramble eggs mixed with American cheese for the twins and slap together peanut butter and jelly sandwiches for the older boys.

Here's what I was thinking: What is *this* life of flipping from Toys R' Us to the pediatrician to Power Rangers to the cupboard for Peter Pan smooth? I used to have a *real* life, or so

I thought—the big job, international travel, a Rolodex crammed with fancy names, clout. Now I was the keeper of four sons and a very wild house. While the eggs sizzled and the boys squealed, the unencumbered Cosmo Girl I loathed while I was her seemed like a romantic figure of freedom compared to the shackled me of Labor Day 1994.

Surreal snippets of yesterday played back as I put Jack and Zane in their high chairs and sat down next to Theo and Isaac at the dining room table. Then, amid the noise of boys and my swinging emotions, I suddenly got very still inside. Wrapped in the gray bathrobe four babies had nestled against while they nursed, my brain started clanging this jubilant message: There are no shackles in this house, this is no jail. These kids are your ticket to freedom like nothing you have ever tasted, the kind that is not hinged on TV appearances or writing for *Life* magazine or being a size 6 again. It's the liberation that comes from the sheer act of living itself. When you stop to be where you are, then your life can really begin.

The Ah Ha's that had come earlier while yelping at the sunrise on a Boulder mountain or in a lotus position in Monterey were blips compared to this epiphany with four children who were shoving lunch in their mouths. It came to me while crouched on the gray carpet picking up cold pieces of scrambled egg and cheese at the foot of Jack and Zane's high chairs. As I scraped harder and harder with my fingernail trying to get every drop of food I started laughing, inexplicably, great gales of laughter that wouldn't stop. Theo and Isaac started laughing, too, then Jack and Zane, who were now throwing egg from their plates down at me. On that gray carpet with egg under my nails and egg in my hair, I realized that for the first time in my life I was exactly where I was supposed to be. On my knees, scraping my babies' lunch off the carpet, bowing to the Great Buddha, humbled, mercifully beaten down by children but exalted, glory God, This Was It!

Flicking my fingernail back and forth I was struck by two things. The journey was over, I was where I belonged. And I seemed to be suspended in time as I scraped hard and long, which was necessary to do a good job, to get all that egg up. These were my children and this was my filthy carpet and I had to be doing what I was doing when I was doing it, however long it took. There was a rightness to being a mother on her knees, scraping and flicking and not thinking about anything else except getting your kids fed and cleaning up after them and Being Where You Are When You Are There. As I washed eight hands and forty fingers and pinned down four wriggly bodies to get them into shorts, T-shirts, socks, and shoes, I remained in the flow of the river of Now that wipes out all anxiety about the past and the future and the Betterment of Self. The Nanny Was Gone but the Mommy Was Here!

Headed to the Washington Hilton pool with four children secured in four car seats in a Chevy Suburban, I absorbed every nuance of Nowness while Theo and Isaac sang "I want to eat, eat, eat apples and bananas" along with Raffi and Zane wailed because the nipple had come off his bottle and he was drenched in peach juice and the scent of Jack's fresh poop wafted toward the driver's seat. After the cacophony of the car came bedlam at the kiddie pool. But the calm that comes from responding without thinking stayed with me as I took part in some fantastic street theater: four boys in yellow inflatable wings splashing and chasing each other, two on foot, two on knees. Isaac pulling out a box of Ritz from my diaper bag and shoving six crackers into his mouth before he chewed. Theo drinking his banana-strawberry Yoplait because I had forgotten to pack a spoon. Jack and Zane drinking the swimming pool. I was alive, fully, in the sun, making sure boys didn't choke, didn't drown, were slathered with sufficient SPF 30 Hawaiian Tropic cream, weren't dripping excrement onto the cement. Bravo!

I had been a member of the Washington Hilton swim club

since the summer of 1984, and those first seasons I used to lie on a chaise all day in a leopard-print bikini and read novels by Dominick Dunne, breaking only to do laps or to get a frozen daiquiri at the poolside cafe. In the summer of 1994, in my black L. L. Bean tank suit frayed at the butt from sitting on cement pool decks holding babies, I was a far different animal that had little to do with come-hither leopard prints or the feather tickles I had learned about in *The Sensuous Woman*.

But it was okay. It was more than okay, it was Everything. I looked to the sky and praised God for allowing me To See: I am the woman who has it all, and it all is swallowing me, crushing me, splicing my mind. And, ironically, in that chaos I found peace. The enormity and immediacy of my responsibilities was giving me what I've been forever grasping at—the ability to simply Be, to surrender to the task at hand, instead of racing past the moment to reach somewhere else. Where can you go when your four children are playing in a kiddie pool? For most of my life I had been so busy becoming, I never experienced what I had when I had it. Recently a Chinese food delivery came with this fortune cookie, which struck me deeply: "The pleasure of what we enjoy is lost by wanting more."

More, more, more. What could be more than watching Isaac hold his breath underwater for the first time? What could be more than Jack and Zane napping side by side in their double stroller, heads touching, matching teddy bear pacifiers bobbing in tandem. There is nothing more than Theo, his little body sticky from a squirting juice box and sweat, hugging me and telling me "You're the best mommy I ever had in my whole life." So this was what I was meant to be after all those years of climbing—I was their mommy, and that was enough. That was too much, really.

Margie Korshak Associates and the *Dallas Times Herald* and United Press International and WETA-TV had once been my identity, had filled me with purpose and direction. People thought I was important; often so did I. But at the core of my success was a gnawing emptiness that wasn't satiated no matter how much glitter was dished my way, a hunger that wasn't even filled while eating lamb chops with Norman Mailer at the Hay-Adams, or sipping tea with Barbara Bush in the vice president's mansion. That line in *Death of a Salesman* describing Willy Loman comes to mind: "You are the saddest, self-centeredest soul I ever did see-saw."

I used to feel as Willy Loman did: ". . . kind of temporary about myself."

With the birth after birth of son after son, I was moving beyond the obsessive self-analysis that had forever racked my heart. Enmeshed in a world of little things and little people, I was slammed into the moment with such ferocity and velocity that now it's all there is. My kids have captured me, and I am surrendering. I am no longer mine; I am theirs.

At Stanford in the mid-1970s I was yearning to rid myself of emotional baggage and cerebral clutter and arrive at that serene destination Ram Dass promises can be ours. As he writes:

"Everybody knows that there is a place which is totally fulfilling. Not a desperate flick of fulfillment. It is a state of fulfillment. You may experience despair that you'll never know that. Good! Because through the despair comes surrender. And through that surrender you get closer to it. And what keeps you from that place that gives you that total feeling, experience, knowing, of fulfillment is all of this posturing, all of your thoughts, all your ways of organizing your world, all of your plans, all of your games."

So this madness in motherhood is the resounding, all-encompassing Now that Ram Dass was speaking of, and I got here without meditation or drugs. I have been forced by four sons who need love and food and who routinely jump off tables to be there now, to be at one with the moment, to be a robot that responds on the split second. Having too much happening all at once has thrust me into pure consciousness. It doesn't feel precisely like Ram Dass bliss, yet I know that I have reached a supreme state of fulfillment. I'm so filled that I'm bursting.

Unlike the identity crises that tracked me through my teens and twenties, I'm no longer concerned with who people think I am, because I'm certainly not that person they have in mind. I know this because I am no longer even the person I thought I was. Here is a snapshot of the Here and Now that magnified my enlightenment on the meaning of existence. Our twins were born. My husband's father died. A steel hook punctured our second son's head to the bone. It missed Isaac's left eye by half an inch. I had a lump that turned out to be benign removed from my right breast.

I will never forget walking into the kitchen for a few seconds and coming out to find Isaac with what looked like a bullet hole between his eyebrows. His brother had accidentally pushed him against a hook on the wall, leaving a black and gaping wound. His blood was everywhere, smeared on his cheeks, on the gray carpet, across my aquamarine blouse. But that moment of madness, and the hours after being stitched up by a plastic surgeon at Georgetown University Hospital, didn't push Chuck and me over the edge, because we were already over the edge— that happened when our litter went from two to four. And once we got home from the hospital, we quickly moved on to the next trauma.

I think of one of my former favorite philosophers, Soren Kierkegaard, and his excruciating mission to figure out life. Kierkegaard had the luxury of spending long, uninterrupted days, even years, trying to uncover the nature of anxiety and despair in relation to self. Here is the type of convoluted insight he came up with, as written in *The Sickness Unto Death*.

"The Despair That Is Conscious of Being Despair and

Therefore Is Conscious of Having a Self in Which There Is Something Eternal and Then Either in Despair Does Not Will It to Be Itself or in Despair Wills to Be Itself."

In sharper years, this stuff that now seems like ramblings from a Martian made perfect sense to me. I, too, once loved to try to decipher my own self and its relation to God and the universe. Dulled by too little sleep and too many children, I lack the motivation to keep wallowing in the Search. Wallowing takes brain power, soul power, time. And frankly, all that thinking in a corner doesn't get you anywhere. It's the perpetual motion of kids that zaps you into Truth.

In those rare moments when four boys and a husband are placated, instead of contemplating philosophy books I now take care of simple animal needs, like reading the new *People*. On the days I am able to accomplish even more, say, paying the phone bill or making a dinner not by Stouffer's, I feel sheer elation.

This raw, primal fulfillment seems strange after an arduous search for identity. However painful the process of exploring the depths of my soul, I relished the uncertainty, the constant strife. After all, angst is a writer's fuel. When our children arrived in a pack and shattered my self-obsessiveness, I should have been miserable. Without a job in daily journalism, a position I had held for more than a decade, who could I possibly be?

My father built a large furniture company over the course of forty years, and just a few months before his retirement he suffered a heart attack. Rather than look forward to the next phase of his life, it filled him with fear. The son of Russian immigrants, he grew up poor in the Depression and had worked in a factory setting most of his life. "What will I do next?" he used to ask. Starting an amusement park in San Diego or teaching business courses at a university were a couple of his ideas. But I do believe that at the age of sixty-seven, the prospect of re-creating himself helped kill him.

In my own re-creation as megamom, there was no time to

lament the transition. Instead, I was flailing in the moment just trying to survive. Here was a typical morning after Nanny No. 2 left and we switched to part-time baby-sitters:

> 5:30 A.M. *Fetch yowling nine-month-old twins, haul fifty-four pounds of Jack and Zane downstairs, bounce them on hips while mashing banana into their oatmeal.*
>
> 6:30 A.M. *Make cheese omelet for two-year-old Isaac, wash twenty baby bottles.*
>
> 7 A.M. *Serve Wheaties to four-year-old Theo, pick pieces of cheese omelet off me, Isaac, and carpet.*
>
> 7:30 A.M. *Get filthy boys cleaned and dressed.*
>
> 8 A.M. *Sit on the kitchen floor entertaining twins with duck puppet while waiting for the extra-strength Mexican coffee to drip.*
>
> 8:15 A.M. *Change three diapers.*
>
> 8:30 A.M. *Stop at grocery store to spend $139 on baby food, diapers, juice, and formula, then drop Theo off at nursery school.*
>
> 9:05 A.M. *Gather Seven Dwarfs and Power Rangers trailed in the living room, read Horoscope in* Washington Post *to see if today is the day someone is going to take me away from all this.*
>
> 9:30 A.M. *Collapse on couch while babies are napping, plunk Isaac in front of* Mary Poppins.
>
> 10:30 A.M. *Fetch yowling twins, fill them with Isomil, then crawl around house after them until it's time to pick up Theo at school.*

By noon, I felt like most people do at midnight. When Chuck got home from work he would herd the boys upstairs for baths, and I'd be left alone in a quiet living room, thinking how futile it is to probe your inner depths for answers on the meaning of life—that the essence of life is the act of living itself. I had grappled enough with the meaning of it all. I had crested on each new cosmic wave. I was sick of probing my psyche. At this age and stage, I wanted to be physical, a Mother Animal buried in, buried by, gyrating flesh. Daily workouts with seven-pound free weights did much for toning my upper body in Dallas. But nothing sculpts muscles like round-the-clock sets of benchpressing twin babies.

I would zoom back to my college days when I frolicked under resplendent blue skies transfixed by a spell of youth and turmoil and San Francisco. I thought of est and of icy swims at Half Moon Bay and carafes of chablis drunk with C.T. or Kelly or John after I got off my waitressing shifts at the New Varsity restaurant. I would remember all that peace I thought I found with books like *Handbook to Higher Consciousness* by Ken Keyes, Jr., who speaks of "continually calming the restless scanning of my rational mind in order to perceive the finer energies that enable me to unitively merge with everything around me."

In my California Wonder Years, I did calm my restless mind, merging with everything around me perched in places like Mount Tamalpais in Marin County. But when enlightenment came, it was fleeting. I was grateful that two decades later, as the New Age was upon us and Healing Your Inner Child became the quest of the 1990s, I didn't get sucked into that writhing inward journey because I was too busy wrestling with many writhing Outer Children. My *Handbook to Higher Consciousness* was no longer necessary; I was as high as I could ever hope to be tumbling with four boys on the ground. I had finally arrived at the Awakened State where you lose awareness of yourself from total immersion in That Which Is Now, the sizzle of turkey bacon, dumped boxes of sixty-four Crayolas.

In the Zen of motherhood I was discovering a lasting joy in the fleetingness of life. At 7:30 P.M., as four tiny bodies lie wedged like puppies between Chuck and me on our king-size bed, I know in my heart that life, however frenetic and mindless, is hopeful and sweet. The relentless climb is over. It was while toiling to reach the top of the mountain that the True Self came knocking, and I found my way back home. Four boys are doing what nothing before them had done; they are securing me close to the kitchen, where I can snack on comfort foods from my own childhood, like Jello pudding layered with bananas and vanilla wafers.

Not that I don't at times miss eating rare tuna and sorbet in restaurants like Nora, where the Clintons like to stop. I miss the tingle of important interviews. It's a kick to have had my interest in alternative medical therapies sparked by Deepak Chopra himself. And when I see Ginger Rogers hoofing it up with Fred Astaire on cable TV, I think of the actress telling me that she was a better dancer than him. Celebrity journalism kept me pumped for years. The kids that came next could keep me pumped for a lifetime.

Something that my friend Norma Babington told me comes to mind. Norma is the mother of three grade-school-age children who left a job in public relations to stay home and raise them. She ended up spending two years as vice-president of their school's PTA, and the following year as president. One Saturday night she and her husband were entertaining a Super Couple, he a lawyer, she a congressional aide, whose kids are taken care of twelve hours a day by an au pair. Norma was talking about all the details she had to attend to as head of the PTA, such as finding spotlights and sound systems for school performances as well as planning Teachers Appreciation Day.

The congressional aide said to her, "Norma, you are so unselfish to do these things for free all the time." Norma didn't respond, but later here's what she was thinking: "What stuck in my head was, no I am not unselfish, I love doing this. I choose to do it, and it's the thing I wanted to do more than anything else in my life. If anything, I'm selfish because we live in a house that is not as nice as it could be and we are driving cars that are not as nice as they could be because I'm not out there making a full-time salary like my husband is. That's so I can be the one who is there when my kids figure out how a puzzle works or when they find their first snail in the backyard."

In my own home, it is emotionally trying at first to break away from the children when they are exploring and playing and eager to show me all their discoveries and feats. But I do eventually pry myself loose and drive off for some much needed time alone, lifted by the sight of them in my rearview mirror, running around the yard with our baby-sitter Mary. On days they are sad, either from illness or just plain kiddie blues, I don't go anywhere, I can't go anywhere, no matter how capable the child-care provider or how important the engagement.

I think of the day a few weeks back when I was all slickered up for a big afternoon and night in Washington, D.C., fifty minutes away, delirious to be escaping. The plan was to first get a haircut at a Georgetown salon, then teach a writing class at American University, and end up at a Mexican restaurant to meet my artist friend Becca Cross for drinks and some grown-up conversation. As I was pulling on my black wool pantsuit with the satin lapels, I was humming and picturing Becca, whose two boys would be home with their baby-sitter, and I eating ceviche and drinking frozen margaritas. We would be feeling feisty and free, without our six sons.

My kindergartner Theo then stuck his head in the bathroom to inform me that he just threw up and his head was "on fire." I took his temperature and the thermometer registered at 103. As I held him in my lap, his sticky face burrowed into my black blazer, I picked up the telephone and called the pediatrician, then canceled the hair appointment with Bertram, the writing class, and the Cactus Cantina date with Becca. I cleaned Theo up and put him in our bed, under our green flannel comforter splotched with all sorts of infant goo fossilized over time.

"Mommy, will you hold me?" Theo asked as he drifted off to sleep.

"Yes, honey," I told him, lying next to him and holding his hot body tightly.

Since the mid-1980s, when yuppies were peaking, talk of striking a balance between parenthood and career has been the central angst of our generation of women. For years I have heard all-stars of the fast track noisily complaining about the juggling act that results from caring for kids and spouse and being addicted to, and stressed out by, success. When I became the mother of four sons, I was certain that for all these long debates among ambitious women on ways to balance our lives, the task was insurmountable—with young children there can be no balance, the scales are tipped toward the children and there's nothing you can do about it. When you give in to that fact real balance comes, the equilibrium you can get only if your psyche and soul are in sync.

I never again want to spend more time in the workplace with strangers than I do at home with family. This dream becomes amplified when I read testimonials from other overachievers, mourning what they have missed.

Reflecting on her hormone-fueled voyage through the decades, Erica Jong admits to some remorse at the mid-century mark. "Now at fifty, when it is too late, I wish I had more children," writes Erica Jong in *Fear of Fifty*. "But when I was fertile, I mostly saw motherhood as the enemy of art and an appalling loss of control. . . . For years, I resolutely remained a writer first, a mother second. It took me the whole first decade of my daughter's life to learn to surrender myself to motherhood. No sooner had I learned that essential surrender than she was entering puberty and I menopause. Years after giving birth, I became a mother against my will because I saw that my daughter needed me to become one. What I really would have preferred was to remain a writer who dabbled in motherhood. . . . But Molly would not permit it. She needed a mother, not a dabbler."

A dabbler mother, those words were a sharp, accusing jab. I was the Dabbling Mom when Theo was first born and I shimmied into a blue-jean skirt and cranberry chenille sweater from the Gap and sat on the "Around Town" TV set locked in heady debate over Robert Mapplethorpe's S&M photographs as if they were icons of globe-shattering importance. Mapplethorpe's shock art, however controversial, means nothing in my teeny cave where everything is important, where you dwell with your children, those invincible shamans of light.

I remained an ace dabbler when Isaac was in my belly and I combed Chicago and Capitol Hill trying to piece together the complicated and wily Dan Rostenkowski. I was the dabbler supreme that summer of unrest as I race-walked the beaches of Delaware with a Walkman blaring Al Green pretending I was twenty-four and at Club Med in Martinique, leaving behind a new nanny to be drowned by My Four Sons.

When I once told a friend all the great journalism I still got to do, even with a bunch of young boys, he said: "What are you avoiding?" I was avoiding my work at home. I was avoiding looking into the eyes of sons who wanted everything and feeling that if I kept giving to them I'd have nothing left for myself. I was avoiding the endless chores that must be done, thanklessly, every day. Restless and wandering all my life, I was avoiding getting stuck in one place too long.

But then came those wondrous crumbs of wisdom—the scrambled egg epiphany on my gray carpet and in my fingernails and the Giddy Knowing that the dabbling could no longer be because four children had strapped me down with ropes like Gulliver's Lilliputians. I was stuck in it, sucked into it, sinking in their adoration and puppy smells. I felt as Ram Dass did when he speaks of his guru from India in *Be Here Now*: "I love him so thoroughly that I would do anything he would ever ask of me. And the highest thing I could think of is being at his feet." Theo and Isaac and Jack and Zane required my Whole and there could be no splintering off from their incessant yanks, no more breaking free from these guys who made me feel as if my heart was always swollen. I Bow to Thee. And as I yielded to this Great Unifying Power, the humans weighting my body and mushing my mind were lifting me, resurrecting me, dousing me in the miracle of Now.

When I am told by their preschool teachers that Theo and Isaac are confident and kind, I am joyous beyond anything I ever felt from journalism awards. What else could you want than kids who are nice? It may help, it just could, you pray it will, to make sound decisions as they grow up in a world where customers are murdered ordering Big Macs at McDonald's and sixth-graders do cocaine. We were having a late lunch in our kitchen when the news broke on television that Yitzhak Rabin had been shot and was in critical condition. Isaac and Theo had a lot of questions as the broadcast unfolded and the announcement came that the Israeli prime minister was dead.

"Mommy, is someone going to hurt us, too?" Theo wanted to know. I told him that I'd protect them as well as I could but that there were bad people in the world who wanted to hurt good people, and that they had to be careful and smart in life. He then asked if there were more good people than bad people. I assured him there were. Isaac smiled, and told his brother not to worry because "Yitzhak Rabin would come back as an angel so he could be with his family again."

Placated by that notion, Theo and Isaac went upstairs to their playroom while Chuck and I stayed in front of CNN, stunned and numb. I was thinking about how a second could change everything, of the membrane separating life and death. During the funeral a couple of days later, the director of Rabin's office read the words of a peace song from a piece of paper that had been in Rabin's pocket when he was shot. It was splattered with the prime minister's blood. I thought of Yitzhak Rabin rising to start a new day, knowing that he was about to speak and sing of peace at a rally, and folding that piece of paper into his pocket so he would know the lyrics. As it turned out, the lyrics were used as his eulogy. Over the course of a few moments and gunshots, Mideast history is rewritten. Life is Now, that's that. You cannot control the evil in the world. All you can control is the tiny universe occupied by your family, and Being There and Loving Them Fully can in turn help them love themselves.

I know that I'm fortunate to be in a profession and marriage that allows me to spend most of each day near my children. But Being There isn't about money or even about staying home full-time. It's about an emotional and spiritual shift, of succumbing to Being Where You Are When You Are, and Being There as much as possible. It's about crouching on the floor and getting delirious over the praying mantis your son just caught instead of perusing a fax while he is yelling for your attention and you distractedly say over your shoulder: "Oh, honey, isn't that a pretty bug."

It's about being attuned enough to notice when your kid's eyes shine so you can make your eyes shine back.

My sister, Fran, a mother of four children ages four months to twelve years, is a partner at a law firm in Chicago. She is devoted to her family and to her work, and she succeeds remarkably well at nurturing both, dividing her time between client meetings, court appearances, school activities and nursing a baby. After a splintered week, she and her husband, Seth, often center their family alone in one place away from the jangle of phones and the maddening pace. On Friday nights, they drive to their cottage on a lake in Wisconsin, where they stay until Monday morning, savoring long meals, reading, playing simple games. The consistency of their ritual has produced a closeknit, healthy family:

"I see our children looking at other families and really treasuring what we have," says Fran. "It's not only important for the kids as the foundation of their lives, but it's also the most grounding influence for me. I see how a sense of security has paid off for the children in their ability to love other people. Because we have a strong family foundation they want to help other people feel more confident about themselves."

Being There Fully is about loving someone more than you have ever loved anyone in your life. Reaching a sublime state with children can come from just staring at them. When I watch my boys sitting next to each other on the couch, huddled under the orange quilt their great-grandmother made, Jack on Theo's lap, Zane's head on Isaac's shoulder, I am overcome by the realization that they all belong to me, that I belong to them. The magnitude of mothering can also be felt in a gesture as simple as the laying on of hands.

Zane is a lead-bodied baby who moves like a bull and is constantly barreling into walls and furniture. His first word was "uh-oh"; his twin's first word was "book." One morning Zane bashed his leg and wouldn't stop howling; he was scared more than hurt. I put him on our bed and started to rub his little, fat leg all over, first at the ankle then slowly moving up the calf to the thigh. Along the way his crying stopped and he melted into a lumpen kitten, staring at me with reverence. Soon he was asleep, and I sat there dumbfounded by my power and by my child's vulnerability.

Isaac frequently screams "Mommy" in a voice that should only be used if there's a fire and I come running to a sheepish toddler, who pleads in a whisper: "I just want you to hold me, Mommy." So I hold him and his head flops on my shoulder and he pats me softly on the back and I wish we could "put today on rewind," like Theo always asks me to do.

I've had some great baby-sitters over the years, but of this I am certain: You and I can have the best caregiver on earth, but there is no one who can physically touch our children like we are able to. That sacred chemistry consoles us, too, it is the optimal soul soother, and it's ours anytime we want. So you might ask yourself the next time you're rushing out of the house: Where are you going? Or are you there already?

I remember the day I picked up the *Washington Post* to the headline that Secretary of Commerce Ron Brown and an entourage of aides and business executives had been killed in a jet crash on a storm-swept Croatian mountaintop. Most of the people on the plane were under the age of forty-four. In an adjacent front-page story, I read that a bearded hermit had been arrested by federal agents in Helena, Montana, suspected to be the terrorist known as Unabomber, responsible for a seventeen-year string of attacks that left three persons dead and twenty-three others severely injured. All the while, my baby Jack was slapping the newspaper for my attention so I could read him the Lillian Vernon catalog that just came in the mail.

"What's this, Mommy? What's this, Mommy?" he asked over and over, as he flipped through the pages and pointed to building blocks and pottery and candles and windsocks. As I listed every item, over and over, I looked into Jack's pale green eyes rimmed with jade. I thought about how he'll be small enough to tuck into my lap like this for only a spell longer. And I was reminded of the innocence of the children I must soon let free into a world that may harm them, make them cynical, perhaps even make them bad. I let the newspaper drop to my feet and buried my face in Jack's neck.

This astonishing day is ours, and on this day we have been assigned as mothers the Herculean task of Being There and loving our families. Tomorrow, as those whose families were torn apart in the driving rains off the Adriatic Sea that blew air force flight T-43A off course can attest, there may not be another chance. We must lavish those we love with our time while we have them. Surely, they are deserving of more of us than our office gets, especially when the payback in this economy is often being downsized out of a job.

"In the current recession, many women have a realistic fear of approaching their bosses for a flexible work arrangement," says Robin Hardman, director of marketing for Families and Work Institute, a New York–based think tank that studies issues relating to the work–personal life balance. "Luckily, an increasing number of organizations are becoming more receptive to new ways of getting work done. In fact, some companies even see a business advantage to keeping their employees happy and less stressed; when employees have greater control over work hours, employers find they get greater productivity."

While there is still a piecemeal approach to family-friendly programs in the U.S. workplace, the changing demographics are pushing corporations to continue to come up with compromises—as we near the end of the century nearly half the U.S. labor force are women. New patterns of employment include flextime, job-sharing, telecommuting, on-site child-care facilities, and opportunities for extended sabbaticals. And the future looks hopeful overall.

Nothing can stop the technological revolution that is making a homecoming possible for increased masses of white-collar workers, not taking them away as was the case throughout industrial history when hands were required to get the job done. With the explosion of access to the Information Superhighway, corporations are now able to decentralize their staffs and set up satellite offices in employee homes. Anyone who has moved her business to a residence can't tell you enough about the benefits—more family time, less stress from commuting and office politics, an expanded sense of control and freedom. I'll add this one from my own experience: you get to sit at your computer in torn sweat clothes from college and you don't have to comb your hair.

"If you really want to find the optimal work-family situation bad enough, you can find it," says William Maddox, vice-president for policy of the Washington-based Family Research Council. "Yes, it is difficult. Yes, there are economic pressures. But if you want to make child rearing your top priority it can be done."

For me, that meant giving up the electric highs that come from daily journalism and a newsroom. But not a day goes by that I'm not elated and inflated for something that occurred because of some ace mothering. Who I am today as Mommy to four is a potent sum total of all the work and play I've done in my life. When you, too, look at all you've accomplished in the past, jobs you've mastered, your strongest life skills, I bet you will see that being a mother to your children is similar to what Queen Noor described about being a queen: "It was all the pieces of my life coming together beautifully." So what if we're queens of only a house and not a country? Everything we were as females and as professionals leading up to maternity—nurturing, intuitive, dogged, durable—prepared us to succeed in this utmost of roles.

In my new position of Militant Mama, all the tools that work so well in journalism have come remarkably into play. To get the story first, fast, and right, reporters must be thorough, vigilant, and resourceful. Here's an example of how all these pieces came together to make for some excellent mothering. After a Passover seder at our temple, Chuck noticed a small tick burrowed into Isaac's groin when he was putting the boys in their pajamas. He pulled out the tick and carried it over to me in our bathroom where I was brushing my teeth. Reared near a river in rural Maryland, Chuck has seen a lot of ticks in his life, and he had this to say: "It's too small to be a dog tick or a wood tick. I think it's a deer tick."

I dropped my toothbrush and immediately called my friend Josette Shiner, who is in remission from full-blown Lyme disease. Josette is the managing editor of the *Washington Times* newspaper and probably knows as much, if not more, about the disease as any doctor in the Southeast, having exhaustively researched treatment options and engineered what appears to be her own cure. She told me three things: Get the tick identified, have Isaac looked at, and do both as soon as possible. Isaac was in the pediatrician's office soon after it opened. Our usual doctor was on Easter vacation, so an associate took a look at the tick under a microscope and at the site of Isaac's bite. He then looked me in the eye, and told me that the tick was a "common wood tick," not a deer tick. I asked him if he was absolutely, positively certain. In a patronizing voice he responded: "I am 100 percent certain that what we have here is a common wood tick. You can stop your worrying." He then assured me that the redness around the bite on Isaac was to be expected, and that we should watch for the high fever that could be a sign of Rocky Mountain spotted fever, a disease transmitted by other ticks.

I asked the doctor for my tick back. He said that after he looked at the tick under the microscope they had discarded it in the infectious waste receptacle. Now it was my turn to look him in the eye, and insist that I still wanted my tick back. So he had the nurse don rubber gloves and fetch my tick out of the trash. When we left the doctor's office Isaac was happy because he got a purple lollipop from the receptionist. But I wasn't happy. There was a pang in my gut, questions in my mind, a compulsion to keep digging. I called the county health department and asked if anyone there could identify ticks. The woman who answered the phone referred me to the Maryland Department of Agriculture. So Isaac and I ended up taking our little brown varmint taped to a glass slide to one of the state's leading entymologists.

Her office had bug posters all over the walls, bug mobiles hung from the ceiling, and a big spider was on her T-shirt. My little boy's eyes were popping out like a fruit fly's as he took it all in. The entymologist held our tick up to the light and said instantly, "It's a deer tick." After she put it under a microscope, she knew more: "It's an adult female black-legged deer tick." By seeking out an insect expert I was able to find out much about the dread deer ticks who spread Lyme: One good piece of news from the entymologist was that it is believed these ticks need to feed at least fifteen hours on a prey to spread the disease. Chuck noticed Isaac's tick the very afternoon he bit.

I called the doctor and told him that for the sake of other mothers who bring in ticks plucked out of their kids—mothers who might not be reporters trained to press for their own answers—he should say the following when faced with this situation again: "I am not an entymologist. I do not know what type of tick this is. Therefore I can only examine your child. I cannot examine your bug." Then I gave him the name of the entymologist we found at the Department of Agriculture as a referral.

Because I followed the female intuition that men often doubt exists but women know to be the source of all truth, I got to the root of things. After consulting with another pediatrician and an infectious disease specialist, we made the decision to give Isaac a course of prophylactic antibiotics. And we now know that every inch of our boys' bodies must be checked before baths because ticks live in the deer- and fox-infested woods around us. I also received reinforcement for what I believed in my gut: nobody knows what a mother knows when it comes to her child, nobody can stretch and push in the Olympian contortions a mother can.

You don't have to be a reporter to pull off a similar performance. All you have to do is trust your heart, and don't let up in any circumstance that threatens your child until you are Absolutely Positively Certain you've done all that you can, until there are no more churning innards pushing you to go on. So what if you offend your doctor? He'll live; your child may not if you don't speak out and take action. There's no stopping the power and effectiveness of a Militant Mama who's trying to do right by her children. As my father used to tell me when I would hesitate to make a move because I was afraid of offending someone: "You're not running for office. Do what you need to do."

That innate Militant Mothering will serve you better than any of the latest findings that come out in parenting studies and articles. You can read all you want on how to raise healthy children, on quality time versus quantity time, on proper ways to punish inappropriate behavior. As I've said before, what is written in your own heart is the best doctrine of all. And if that heart clenches in pain each time you leave for work in the morning and you're noticing that your children won't stop clinging to you whenever you are around and the split in your soul is too agonizing to take anymore, then move on, give up, surrender to that ancient wisdom you were given as a gift when you were born female.

I urge you to follow the sentiment of an advertisement I stumbled across in a health magazine for the Graduate School for Holistic Studies in Orinda, California: "Align Your Career with the Vision of Your Heart." It may take some scurrying and disappointment, but keep trying. Finding a job that gives you more time with your children is the most important task you can expend energy on. It may mean whittling down, even walking away from, your hard-earned profession. But it also means assuring that your children are protected and loved by the human being who can protect and love them better than anyone else. May the memory of my Passover tick serve you well, it surely is serving me well: The bug preserved in a tiny glass vial of alcohol now lives in my purse so I can be reminded every day of what I can do, of what I need to do, of the value of my job at home.

I listened with a heavy heart as a local doctor shared with me the conflict she feels in her inflexible and demanding field. Annapolis obstetrician Lauren Rogers, thirty-three, mother of an infant and a three-year-old, must spend all day in an office or in the hospital. Her patients need her hands, computers can't pull babies out. Ironically, this woman who translated her love of children into a career is giving most of her time to the off-spring of others. She calls her nanny "constantly" to find out what's going on with her own kids, wishing she could dash home when she liked instead, or work half days. But flextime is hard to come by in the competitive specialty of obstetrics. Dr. Rogers says many of her colleagues actually hold in disdain peers who take off more than six weeks for maternity leave, that a month is deemed sufficient.

The unwritten rule of her profession is this: as a physician who does surgery in a specialty that is rapidly advancing you must consistently be in the operating room in order to maintain your skills and evolve as a state-of-the-art player. How long a Dr. Mom can keep this up is an individual choice based on emotions and finances. Here's how two of my non-physician friends chose to make the money they needed to help their families while making the time they needed to spend with their children.

Holly Eddy, forty, is the mother of six-year-old Chelsea, three-year-old Smythe, and is expecting a baby any day. At different junctures of her career in retail she was an assistant buyer at Bloomingdale's in New York and a buyer for Brody's department store in North Carolina. After more than a decade in her field, she stopped working when she became pregnant with her first child.

One of Holly's favorite venues to shop for children's

clothes was the Big Enough catalog, and when she was expecting for the second time she inquired during a phone order if there was a way she could get involved. The Big Enough owners asked her to become a home-show representative—that is, to stage trunk shows of the clothes each season in her home and invite friends and neighborhood women to buy direct from her living room. Three years later, she now covers the Washington, Maryland, and Virginia region and is Big Enough's top representative out of the hundred they have in place across the country. Each season so far, Holly has been able to drum up an additional $5,000 in sales, of which she gets a cut.

Continuing to soar in the retail business she adores doesn't mean diminished time with the children; Chelsea and Smythe are at every show, modeling the clothes for potential customers. Holly's income from Big Enough covers the children's tumbling and dance classes, soccer league fees and vacations, activities her middle-class family would not be able to afford if they were solely dependent on her husband's salary as a computer specialist. During the six years I've known Holly, she has never had to spend money on child care—the girls are either in school or with her.

A gourmet chef and ace menu planner, Fiona Bryson, thirty-eight, also wanted and needed to make some money but she dreaded the notion of leaving her two children, ages six and three, in the hands of a day-care center or baby-sitter. So this is the schedule she cooked up with the Palate Pleasers caterers in Annapolis: Fiona goes into the storefront shop on Tuesdays and Thursdays from 4 A.M. to 11 A.M., and on Saturdays from 4 A.M. until noon to prepare bakery items such as scones, muffins, and desserts. She also does private dinner parties in clients' homes one night a weekend. While Fiona is pleasing palates, her husband is in charge of the children.

She says it is "totally necessary" for the financial stability of the family for her to bring in additional income: "We could barely squeak by on only my husband's salary." Fiona's work is also totally necessary for her emotional health: "Being out with people in the world and not only with children in the house keeps me sane." Granted, getting up at 3 A.M. to be on the job by 4 A.M. isn't a schedule for everyone, but what Fiona gets back from driving across town before dawn is full days that revolve around her children, not her profession.

A year ago an author friend, Lynne Olson, stopped me cold one morning with a telephone call to tell me her twelve-year-old daughter Carly had been diagnosed with a brain tumor. Lynne was a tenure-track professor in the School of Communication at American University and in the midst of coauthoring a book with her husband, Stanley Cloud, called *The Murrow Boys*, on Edward R. Murrow and the origin of CBS news. We talked about CAT scans and brain surgeons and second opinions and the children we love so much we can't imagine going on without them. I told her that when I almost lost Theo I found my real purpose in life, To Take Care of Him.

During five hours of surgery, Carly's suspicious mass turned out to be a nonmalignant growth of abnormal tissue that will not hamper Carly's development if it remains the same size. But Lynne's world was changed forever. After what she called "the worst month of my life" thinking her only child might be terminally ill, she eventually made the decision to focus on what she loves most, her daughter and writing books, and leave her prominent post at American University.

"The one thing you think you can count on is the health of a child," says Lynne. "And when you can't count on that it shows you that nothing is settled in this world and you better go after today what you think is the most important."

Captured by Children, Free at Last

Too many graying baby boomers who have delayed motherhood for careers are now finding themselves making last-ditch efforts to achieve through technology what has been romanced for centuries as the fruition of our femininity. More than 36,000 children in the United States have been born as the result of assisted reproductive techniques. We all know several of these women in our own social groups who are part of what the September 1991 *Time* magazine cover story called "an infertility epidemic" that hasn't shown signs of letting up.

We hear stories of painful and costly fertility treatments, precarious adoption procedures, and emotional upheaval with each botched attempt. The plight of one of my oldest friends, Simone Gould, is unfortunately not an isolated example. She is a success in the advertising field, but because of infertility, a sense of loss and failure shadowed her for years.

Simone conceived twice through in vitro fertilization, at $10,000 a try, only to lose both pregnancies, one at five months, the other at five weeks. This came after nine unsuccessful artificial insemination attempts. Throughout the process, she suffered through rubber-band cycles of psychological devastation each time a friend announced she was expecting, and consistently black and blue buttocks from the two-and-a-half-inch-long needle she used to inject herself with egg-inducing hormones. Finally, in December 1995, the Goulds adopted a baby girl, after being on edge throughout the birth mother's pregnancy to see if she would change her mind. Now, Simone, the owner of an art studio that produces illustrations for television commercials, doesn't allow Madeline out of her sight. She has set up a nursery in her downtown Chicago studio, complete with crib, swing, and changing table.

"I didn't wait forty-one years to have a baby to leave her with someone else," says Gould.

At some point in your flaring career, you, too, have to stop and ask yourself: What is the most important thing in my life? And if the answer is your children, then live like that. Make them your center. There is nowhere higher to go. This is the Consummate Job. When the children come first and you come second, you won't be parents who drive their children to college to start freshman year then sob the whole way home because it went too fast and you missed most of it because of office bullshit that eats up weeks and years without your even realizing it. Why give your all to a corporation when children are hungering for you at home, as much as they can get, possibly more than they are getting?

This does not mean you have to be home 100 percent of the time. This does mean that you should be there as much as you can.

In the words of my friend Florence Wiedemann, a magical and wise Jungian psychologist in Dallas: "The most important gift you can give to the world is to produce quality humans who are richly endowed with feelings and ideas and compassion. And that takes time."

Time: "A person's experience during a particular period," reads a definition in the dictionary. How and what you experience in an instant of time is a tidy summation of all of life: all you ever have, really, is what you feel inside at the moment you are feeling it. I think of the blurred moments that many people experience, that I experienced, as an employee of companies where what you did yesterday and what you do tomorrow is where your value lies. The minutes whip by on the clock, rarely to be registered as precious events unto themselves in your heart. With four kids, and eighty fingernails and toenails to clip, the minutiae of the day now breaks down into subtleties-in-the-second that can seem like eternities. When I did the est training in 1976 I was promised that "est will transform your ability to experience." It did not, nor did any of my numerous other stopovers on spiritual bandwagons as a personal-growth groupie. Finally, twenty years later that transformation has occurred, catalyzed by the Anthony boys and the nuances of ordinary life, not quick-fix gurus. Because of these children I am constantly made aware of the extraordinary in the ordinary.

On this February morning I am walking with Theo and Isaac and Jack and Zane at Harbour Center, an outdoor shopping mall. We stroll by a woman about my age wearing a short black skirt and a maroon blazer with gold buttons. She is sitting on a bench and talking in an authoritative tone on a palm-sized cellular phone. I notice that she is wearing a wedding ring. We park our stroller nearby and I open up a bag of bagel and cream cheese sandwiches and pass them out to the boys. As they chew and howl, I can't take my eyes off the woman or stop wondering what is she working on. My curiosity really gets going when I hear pieces of a conversation that allude to "six million last quarter" and "restructuring the East Coast."

After ten minutes or so I crumple up the white paper bag, toss it in the garbage, and we leave this mystery woman and her mystery job. We continue to stroll on the sidewalk in front of the storefronts, stopping to ogle the display of swimsuits the color of lime sherbet at South Moon Under and the science toys in the window of Zany Brainy. We pass teenagers in ripped blue jeans and baseball caps on backwards and a mother holding a newborn in a Snugli that has a red balloon tied to it. The sun is warm and the clouds are cotton puffs and my kids are all talking at once and they have chapped faces smeared with cream cheese. Nothing sensational is happening but everything feels sensational. I turn back to the woman on the bench, with a phone at her ear.

On the car ride home we stop in front of a neighbor's house and watch their brown-and-white cows eat grass. The boys are shouting "Moooo, moooo," but I'm still caught up in that woman on her lunch break who wasn't on any kind of break at all. And I'm thinking about all she missed in that hour at Harbour Center, the Here and Now that is gone in a finger snap. That thought remained with me throughout an afternoon when I'm conscious of everything that happens when it is happening, a span of time when I am held captive in the present's deep embrace.

Lunch starts and Jack tips over a large bowl of Uncle Ben's Instant Rice, sending it from one end of the kitchen to the other. I scoop it up with my hand, the twins on my back. They ask for grapes, and to safeguard against choking, I peel each one and slice them into quarters. Isaac starts crying because he can't find the plastic egg for his Silly Putty. I retrieve it from under his bed, come downstairs, and the Silly Putty is in his hair. After the last gummy trace has been removed, we cram together on the love seat in the kitchen and I open our ninety-six-page *Disney's Pocahontas* book. In the beginning I'm wishing that I had instead grabbed *One-Minute Bible Stories* from the shelf, but soon I'm getting into it, as I point out each bird, each leaf, each butterfly, every color. When I get to the part when Pocahontas has taken John Smith into the forest I am reading to four gaping statues:

"As they ran through the trees, Pocahontas showed him how all the parts of nature—animals, plants, the wind, the clouds, even people—are alive and connected to each other. Her words and the importance of what she showed him so touched his heart that Smith was changed."

I look at my boys hypnotized by their mommy and pray that nothing ever changes for us. And at the end of the story, as Pocahontas is watching the man she loves sail away, a prism of leaves swirling around her, Theo says he is sad for her. So I introduce the concept of unrequited love and pass on some wisdom that the Rolling Stones taught me: "You can't always get what you want, but if you try sometimes you get what you need." When I close the book a full hour has passed and I'm thinking that whoever invented *One-Minute Bible Stories* and other One-Minute books for children must be one very busy person.

And so the rest of the day goes. Wiping banana off the TV screen. Scrubbing the oak kitchen counter to remove the stains of indelible black marker. Taking apart a musical place mat so it will stop playing "Twinkle, Twinkle Little Star" over and over and over. Putting a Ninja Turtle transformer back together. Scraping mud off four pairs of sneakers with my Swiss army knife. Mixing leftover rice on plates with leftover ground beef from last night for tonight's dinner. Dicing cantaloupe. Loading the dishwasher, turning it on, closing my eyes and imagining its whirring is massaging me all over—until I'm interrupted by Jack clanging a tambourine at my knees.

When evening comes and I'm watching the amber of sunset on the river and Chuck has the four boys in one bathtub I feel as if I really did something that day. I'm breathless, really, from all there is to absorb and do during one minute and one hour when you are cornered by kids and life. I feel like Henry David Thoreau must have felt when he wrote this in *Walden*: "[T]he whole body is one sense, and imbibes delight through every pore."

And I know when I'm carrying the twins—Jack in one arm and Zane in the other—to their cribs, and their freshly washed hair is downy under my chin, that I did the best I possibly could that one day in my one life. I cherish having child care available when deadlines loom and appointments beckon. But Lord, do I covet those days when there's no one else around, and there's nothing else to do but be on my own with my kids.

Oriana Fallaci's anthology of political profiles, *Interview with History*, features an interview with Golda Meir in which the late Israeli prime minister talks about what she gave up at home in order to run a country. Meir has just told Fallaci that to be successful, "a woman has to be much more capable than a man."

"Doesn't that perhaps mean it's more difficult to be a woman than a man?" Fallaci asks her.

"Yes, of course," responds the prime minister. "After all, it's the woman who gives birth. It's the woman who raises the children. And when a woman doesn't want only to give birth, to raise children . . . when a woman also wants to work, to be somebody . . . well, it's hard. Hard, hard. I know it from personal experience. . . . Such a struggle breaks out in you, your heart goes to pieces . . . it's all running around, trying to be in two places at once, getting upset . . . well, all this can't help but be reflected on the structure of the family. Especially if your husband is not a social animal like yourself and feels uncomfortable with an active wife, a wife for whom it's not enough to be only a wife. . . . There has to be a clash. And the clash may even break up the marriage. As happened to me. Yes, I've paid for being what I am. I've paid a lot.

"I know that my children, when they were little, suffered a lot on my account. I left them alone so often. . . . I was never with them when I should have been and would have liked to be. Oh, I remember how happy they were, my children, every time I didn't go to work because of a headache. They jumped and laughed and sang, 'Mamma's staying home! Mamma has a headache!' I have a great sense of guilt toward Sarah and Menachem, even today when they're adults and have children of their own . . . still I have to be honest and ask myself, Golda, deep in your heart do you really regret the fact that you behaved as you did with them? No. Domestic bliss wasn't enough for me. I had to be doing what I was doing!"

Later in the Fallaci interview Golda Meir admitted that after nearly thirty years of public service, she was "exhausted." And that perhaps there was something more to quest after:

"I can't go on with this madness forever," the Israeli prime minister continued. "If you only knew how many times I say to myself: To hell with everything, to hell with everybody, I've done my share, now let the others do theirs, enough, enough, enough.

"I like to be with nothing to do, even just sitting in an armchair, or wasting time with little things I enjoy. Cleaning the house, ironing, cooking a meal. . . . I'm an excellent cook, I'm an excellent housewife. I like to be with people, to talk about this and that—to hell with serious talk, political talk! I like to go to the theater. I like to go to the movies, without my bodyguard underfoot. How did it happen that whenever I want to see a film, they even send the Israeli army reserves along with me?

"This is a life? . . . I'm a grandmother. I don't have many more years to live. And I intend to spend those years with my grandchildren. . . . I should be the master of the clock, not the clock the master of me."

Golda Meir was interviewed in Jerusalem by Oriana Fallaci in November 1972. The following year she left office after accepting responsibility for Israeli casualties from Egyptian and Syrian forces during the 1973 Yom Kippur War, stemming from her country's lack of preparedness. Then, Golda Meir finally got her wish of retiring to her kitchen, and close to her grandchildren. She moved back into her little house on a quiet street in Ramat Aviv where she lived next door to her son and his family until she died of lymphoma on December 8, 1978, at the age of 80. Unfortunately, it is impossible to know how well you can thrive away from the zenith of power until too much of your life has been consumed by it. That realization comes clearest to those who are old or sick.

I was especially moved by a *Life* magazine article written on former chairman of the Republican National Committee Lee Atwater when he was dying of brain cancer: "I acquired more wealth, power and prestige than most. But you can acquire all you want and still feel empty. What power wouldn't I trade for a little more time with my family? What price wouldn't I pay for an evening with friends? It took a deadly illness to put me eye to eye with that truth, but it is a truth that the country, caught in its ruthless ambitions, can learn on my dime."

How about my own ambitions? There are glaring reminders of the cost of the climb. On weekdays I write in my office between 8:30 A.M. and 11:30 A.M., while Theo and Isaac are at preschool and the twins are careening through the house, tailed by our baby-sitter Mary. At some point each morning my eyes land on the stacks of boxes holding twenty years of taped interviews, hundreds of recordings with movie stars, politicians, fashion designers, artists, a First Lady, a queen, and Billy Graham, the most revered evangelist in the world. And I am always reminded of what is missing among these relics of the Glitter Age—a tape of Theodore J. Krasnow. I never did sit down with him and prod him about the things I asked all my subjects, questions that centered on faith and family and mission. When my dad was midway into a great story about his past, I would always think of stopping him and running to get my tape recorder, but then I'd put it off, knowing there would be another time. But that time never came and I will always be left wondering how my father developed an interest in furniture-making or if he believed in God or why he married my mother.

When friends tell me they haven't seen their aging parents in months I urge them to fly home immediately and ask them everything they ever wanted to know as if it were their last chance, however sensitive it may be to pick through family history. If there's something you want to learn or say, Today Is the Day, now is the time.

I interviewed my mother soon after my father died and she told me, in gruesome detail, her story of surviving in Nazi-occupied Paris during World War II. We've got that tape forever, for our children, for their children.

Family and friends are all you ever really have, it's the one thing you can claim—all else is sideline fluff that you try to own or to tame but in the end is temporal, it leaves you, it lets you down—those jobs that Mean Everything, social games, tortured loves such as mine with Timothy, who I insisted on spending Christmas 1985 with instead of with my own family. My father asked me to spend the holidays in Chicago, but I was afraid of killing my chances with my born-again boyfriend, so instead I met him in Seattle at the home of his unwelcoming parents, who were aghast that this Jewish girl was set upon their son. They were right that we were wrong. I should have been where I belonged, in a loving nest with my mother and my father, who would be dead in two months, and who spent his last holiday season watching old home movies of his young children on vacation in Tucson. With an eye fixed on the horizon, I had missed what was right in front of me. Theodore, Isaac, Jack, and Zane, my wriggly little boys, luckily have me imprisoned in the fleeting moment that is now.

Only this Now with the Children isn't a cage at all. It's the marrow; finally, I have drilled and drilled right to the Essence. What I could never have imagined way back then when watching my own mother smoking and sighing in the kitchen was that being a housewife would someday be liberating for me. After years of dealing forcefully in the world as an octopus juggling, and often dropping large pieces of a complicated and sophisticated life, kitchen duty actually came as a gigantic relief. I am no longer glued to the TV talk shows or newspaper headlines for fodder on national trends and personalities to pitch as articles to magazines. The breaking stories I am most interested in can be found in the calendar section of the free weekly *Chesapeake Family*, where I can find out when the circus is coming to town.

Even if I wanted to escape the intense hold of my sons, there's no way really. On one recent and rare outing alone, I reached in my purse for my car keys and accidentally squeaked a rubber dolphin. I got in the driver's side and sat on some potato chips. I started up the car and there was a pink Power Ranger next to the accelerator. The smell of rotten milk was coming from somewhere in the backseat. I ended up at a sidewalk cafe to meet my friend Judy Billage for lunch, and at the table next to us a baby boy was crying, an insistent, familiar wail that made me feel like ditching my chicken Caesar salad and running home.

I would never have dreamed in 1975 as a junior at Stanford fired up by radical feminism that two decades later I would be warmed to the heart by calling for delivery of an extra-large, extra-cheese pizza under the name of "Mrs. Anthony." I picture how the guy answering the phone is picturing me as he tries to understand my order above the shrieks in my kitchen—a harried mom with a baby in her arms. I like that picture, it is basic and good. And I would never have believed that it would make me feel strong and safe each time a piece of mail comes addressed to our home as Mr. and Mrs. Charles E. Anthony III, this after resenting the fact that my own mother's name on letters was always shrouded in Mr. and Mrs. Theodore J. Krasnow. After floating solo for so long and searching far and wide for something to grab on to, being at one with a family and forgetting about trying to be one with an illusory cosmos and Supreme Being I could never quite reach is the greatest relief of all.

When I was thirty-one I interviewed the eighty-six-year-old sculptor Louise Nevelson, and I remember feeling envy when she told me "I always knew exactly who I was and exactly what I wanted." I did not know until my fortieth birthday hit. And now I know who and what I am, what I was meant to do and be. I am a mother happily humbled by her batch of boys, a woman who needs more than anything else to love, and be loved, by a family that is hers. I am a woman who believes that God has come through for her.

The ambition that raged in my twenties and thirties remains at my core. Yet the force that propelled my career is now the energy field making my boys better. So I admit to still being a Type A consumed by her work, only now my primary work is them. From watching them grow and learn and love each other, I am complete, I have arrived, this is the peace I wanted to feel. All this makes me wistfully aware that being a mother to young children is the Best Self I have ever had, that I may ever have. For after all my far-flung escapades, I have proven to be a woman who draws her deepest satisfaction from sticking close to home.

But who can predict this stuff when you are young? All you knew in the 1970s at the peak of the women's movement was that you didn't want to grow up to be like your mother. Yet I have grown up to be like Helene Krasnow. This mother, who used to snap our window shades open at 7 A.M. and serve breakfast at 7:15 A.M. and lunch at noon and dinner at 5 P.M. and have us in bed by 8 P.M., raised a daughter who has four children on an identical schedule, a daughter with a wet kitchen towel flung over her shoulder. My mother did not cry when her children left for college because she knew she didn't miss anything. In fact, she was more than ready for the next stage to begin. When all three of us were out of the house, the first thing she did was to get out of the house, too, taking a job as a saleswoman at Lord & Taylor on Michigan Avenue, where she still works to this day in the menswear department, at the age of seventy-five.

She goes to the store in silk scarves and pearl earrings and navy blue blazers and gray wool skirts while I am at home in a black velour pantsuit that I sleep in, carpool in, wear to Safeway. I envy her being Of the World, she envies me being swarmed by needy children. "This too shall pass," she always tells me, and I'm aware of her message, that soon enough I'll be someone else again, so will she. Being on her feet all day is beginning to wear her out. I know that I can't freeze this Mother Self of Now that has me captivated by its perfection, that it, too, will float down the river of time.

As autumn is passing a wave of change is already taking place. In the span of two weeks, Theo lost his first tooth, rode his bicycle without training wheels, and learned to tie his shoes. My baby Isaac is now a toddler who says things like "Mommy, do you think if I got a big enough ladder I could climb through the clouds and kiss God's face and touch the moon?" Our twins who were born yesterday know how to vacuum and call me "Iris."

I often heard my own mom say that her fondest memories are of when we were small and sitting around our Formica kitchen table watching "Bozo's Circus" and eating a lunch she had made. She explained that with three children a year and a half apart she was so busy she never had time to think. She always ends her nostalgic meanderings with a solemn shake of the head, a sigh, and "Where did the time go?" I look at my own boys mashing cereal into their mouths and bask in the glorious present that too soon shall pass. I relish the perpetual fullness gained from the care and feeding of gooey children and never catching my breath until I hit the bed at 9 P.M.

I am blatantly reminded of how quickly it goes as I hold three-year-old Isaac on a helicopter ride at Funland in Rehoboth Beach, Delaware, and I remember the helicopters at Kiddie Land near Oak Park and my father in the seat next to me, as if it was last weekend—not thirty-five years ago. The life cycle revolves in one, swift circle.

So I can't stop little boys with silky cheeks who are molded to their mother from changing into reticent adolescents with stubble. Soon, so soon, they will not need me to wrap them in worn yellow blankets and sing silly songs and rock them to sleep.

I can't stop Theo and Isaac and Jack and Zane, who loop limbs on the floor as if they were one creature, from venturing off in four directions to different colleges instead of all ending up at Georgetown University or American University an hour away—my fantasy. I have no assurance that we will marry four sons on our bluff overlooking the Severn River in front of the shingled house their father built. But I can dream, and I can thank God for Now.

Right Here, Right Now, I'm suspended in a moment so holy that it has replaced my spiritual wanderlust. The single-mindedness of this mission to Be There for the boys brings my God closer, makes me know that it doesn't get more blessed than this. In years gone by I would gaze toward heaven, throw up my hands, and plead with the Lord to take me, to find me. I have kept the December 1990 issue of *Life* with the question "Who Is God?" on its cover of a night sky ablaze with stars. The article featured testimonies from twenty-three persons on how God appears to them. I read that magazine when it first came out and Theo was about to celebrate his first birthday, and I stopped on this line from Hollywood producer and mother Lynda Sparrow: "Hannah's my evidence that God exists," she said of her daughter. I knew what she meant then and I know more what she means now: Four children assure me every second that the Divine resides right on the ground. Finally, God is no longer a Spirit Beyond that I am desperate to reach. That Force is everywhere I am.

God is on the stoop of our house with Isaac as water drips on his head from the flower box overhead and he's wearing a Simba hat with floppy ears and his chipped front tooth shows through a cocky smile. God is with me as I'm swaying Zane on one hip to "One Two Three O'Clock Rock," while mopping up apple sauce around Jack in his high chair who is thumping to the beat with his spoon on his Little Mermaid plate. God is in my Chevy Suburban while crusty-nosed Jack and Zane and Isaac are napping in their car seats all in a row and Theo is next to me asking "Mommy, when you're one-hundred ten how old will I be?" God is with me as I knead clumps out of thirty steamy sweet potatoes with my hands preparing for a large Thanksgiving dinner at a juncture of time that I'm so thankful I fall on my knees.

God is guiding our marriage and reminding me when the road gets rough that this could be As Good as It Gets. God has elevated me to heights I never dreamed possible by bringing my Judaism back. In Washington, D.C., we belonged to a mammoth synagogue with marble floors and a motorized ark and a membership of 3,100 families. One of the best discoveries after moving was a tiny temple, housed in a peeling stucco building with a leaky roof and sputtering furnace and a membership roster of 250 families who sit on plastic stacking chairs during services. In a span of less than a year, I have become a temple officer, chair of the nursery school committee, and, with several other congregants, spent a Sunday morning building a white picket fence in front of the playground. Feeling the earth and hammering in stakes to fortify our House of God was exhilarating.

I am my mother, that ruling force of Hadassah at West Suburban Temple in Oak Park in the 1960s.

It's this religion of action in the every day that makes me serene and centered, a long-awaited Oneness after a tortuous search to know God up close and personally. I'm convinced now that you can't know God really. You can try. You should try. But it's a path, not a destination. What you can know is your children. You can try to know your spouse. You can mash potatoes. You can find sheets on sale at Sears. And from this mastery of the immediate comes more religion than you will ever need. So I am finally home in my spirituality, and God has never seemed nearer. This came not from Blasts from the Above but from the interconnectedness of my family and friends, like the women in the raucous book club I've been in since 1988, and

Terri Rubin in Colorado, a sister since the summer of 1965 at Camp Agawak. If religion is that thing that gets a hold on your heart and doesn't let go, then I had discovered God through the people I loved most.

So I'm no longer boring around in my brain for answers on the ancient rift between Christianity and Judaism, or desperate to come face-to-face with God. I can't do it anymore, my mind is not what it once was, I admit it, and my soul is no longer starving. What I do know as Truth without any thinking at all is that my faith has been reborn in the dilapidated Little Shul on the Prairie sited on eleven acres of open land where we are making things happen for the community, and where I am constantly reminded of who I really am, a woman riveted by the power of the Shema, the spoke of my people:

"And you shall love the Lord your God with all your heart, and with all your soul, and with all your might. And these words which I command you today shall be upon your heart. And you shall teach them to your children, and you shall talk of them when you sit in your house, and when you go on the way, and when you lie down, and when you rise up."

So it's come full circle—after yogic postures and Vedic chants and transcendent glimpses of enlightenment on nude California beaches and Colorado cliffs, the spiritual blast that hits me the hardest comes from saying the blessings with other families at a Hanukkah dinner in the temple's basement social hall, and breaking up pieces of potato latkes for my boys. From this mundane and messy scene comes the "great fullness of being" Buddhist master Sharon Salzberg writes of in *Loving Kindness: The Revolutionary Art of Happiness*. As she describes it: "To be undivided and unfragmented, to be completely present, is to love. To pay attention is to love."

To be present and love wholly—indeed I was finding that simple formula was at the heart of happiness.

I feel this when I'm lying next to Chuck in the grass, and

suddenly the kids, holding buckets of water, lope down the hill toward us, Zane then Jack then Theo then Isaac, the sun lighting their blond hair to look like halos. They dump water on our heads then jump on our backs. And there we are, a family above a river, muddy and tangled and wet. And all I had to do to tap into what feels like the quintessential life force is Be There. They Make Me Feel Like a Natural Woman, Oh, Babies, What You've Done to Me. Sprigs of gray in my hair and lines around my eyes, I know that my forties are going to be ripe and right, with nothing separating me from life.

·For the first time ever, there is no one out there whose job I want. Many of the people whose jobs I wanted no longer even want their own jobs. I compare notes all the time with Tom Ferraro, my closest comrade from United Press International. He is forty-seven years old and has never been married. We remember writing about national trends and global leaders in the smoke-filled newsroom full of hard-charging reporters slumped over their computer terminals, chain-smoking, swearing, never letting up on a story, like dogs chewing bones.

Tom was one of the star reporters of UPI with a legacy of formidable pieces. He traveled with an undercover narcotics agent through the drug-infested streets of southeast Washington, spent several days at a Hari Krishna village in West Virginia under investigation for a murder, accompanied troops into the fields of Iraq and Kuwait during the Persian Gulf ground war. The year Theo was born and I left my desk at UPI for the toy stores, Tom became White House correspondent, a position that meant he got to golf with President Bush.

He visits a lot and our boys heap onto his lap and he tickles their stomachs and buys them wonderful treats like a red schoolhouse music box. After thirty years of dating different women, Tom says he may be ready for kids and a wife, but that daily journalism is "addictive" and it's a habit that gets in the way of a traditional personal life. "I started at UPI when I was twenty-four, and then I thought I'd be twenty-four for the rest of my life. Suddenly, I looked in the mirror and I was in my mid-forties."

Martha Sherrill, one of the best and most prolific profile writers in the country, got winded before her fortieth birthday. After ten years in the Style section of the *Washington Post*, ten marathon years of rotating subjects interviewed in rotating cities, she "woke up one morning" and realized that she didn't want to travel for the newspaper anymore. This woman who has interviewed everyone from John F. Kennedy Jr. to Madonna had found there was no one else out there she just had to get to, no story she just had to write.

"I didn't want to interview Jeffrey Dahmer. I didn't want to cover earthquakes and riots, or go to Africa and write about a diminishing tribe," says Sherrill. "I started to realize what I had given my bosses of myself, not only my life, but my freshness, my innocence, that I had become jaded. And that was a lot to give up to somebody."

She says part of her decision to stay still for a while has to do with the fact that she is now in a promising relationship that she has no desire to run away from. "You start thinking, 'Am I going to get married and have children, or am I going to go on having this crazy life forever?' I'll tell you, this crazy life I've been leading for the past ten years, I started to feel like an urban vampire, like I've been doing it for a hundred years. There is so much else I want my life to be about. I love to garden. I love just being in my house."

As I put together a zucchini quiche in my kitchen I think about the White House press conference on international drug abuse I covered for UPI, when I was three inches away from Nancy Reagan, and I remember my cozy tea with Barbara Bush when she revealed her lust for Mexican food. I've never met Hillary Clinton; there's a good chance I never will. As I chop zucchini and form crusts my mind wanders to my friends with their plastic press passes dangling from chains around their necks that get them into the highest places in Washington. My press tags expired in 1989. Then my consciousness shifts to my hands and the Pyrex bowl and the knife and how the deep green of the vegetables is the same mystical green of the pine trees out the window. And I'm struck by how laborious making a quiche actually is, from shredding the cheddar with a hand-grater to slicing the zucchini and mushrooms, then layering it all together, artfully, one piece at a time.

Throughout the process I realized I wasn't thinking of anything else—I was just moving my hands like a sculptor, pressing and forming and cutting. Quiche is a dish I make often and well, but something was different this December day. I wasn't rushing through it haphazardly; I was arranging it, alternating the right size slice of mushroom with a corresponding slice of zucchini, delicately sprinkling cheese as if tossing fairy dust, instead of hurriedly flinging it on in a clump, pouring the egg mixture slowly so it doesn't spill over the edges. Those quiches came out like cover shots for *Gourmet*, their insides masterful masonry. I smiled hugely. For a life that was forever measured in grand accomplishments, baking beautiful vegetable pies is certainly not a grand feat. But that's what it has come down to; the perfect quiche was as big as anything I had done in weeks. I was enveloped in the folds of universality described in Shunryu Suzuki's *Zen Mind, Beginner's Mind*: "[W]hen you do something, you should do it with your whole body and mind; you should be concentrated on what you do. You should do it completely, like a good bonfire. You should not be a smoky fire. You should burn yourself completely. If you do not burn yourself completely, a trace of yourself will be left in what you do."

I looked at my hands, etched with fissures from soapy water and Baby Wipes. I love the feel of these hands in mud or in child flesh or in brownie batter. I love how tranquillity takes hold when the hands take over. I know what Ram Dass knows when he writes in *Be Here Now*: "It feels like the first real thing that's ever happened to me! Everything else had a certain hustle like quality to it." I think of the bamboo craftsmen in Japan who weave magnificent baskets for drying shiitake mushrooms; the Zuni tribes who inlay slivers of coral and turquoise into jewelry. If I get lost in the creation of a couple of measly quiches they must be inhabitants of the Purest State of All as they move their fingers for ten-hour stretches and empty their minds along the way. These hands of mine that for so long were manicured and holding goblets of champagne are now usually steeped in food and filth. I love these chapped hands, with their ragged cuticles and broken nails.

And, oh, God, how I laugh with love at our Isaac the angel with my father's face who gets so excited about what's to come that he asks me nearly every day, "Mommy, is it tomorrow today?"

In Cosmo-Girl gallivanting years gone by, it took major stuff to send me—making out in front of the Eiffel Tower, traveling alone to Marrakech, floating in the Dead Sea. Today it's the little things that get me. One recent afternoon I was filling up my Suburban with Regular at the Shell station in my neighborhood, and a vision ten yards away made me suddenly grow teary. The sight that set me off was—get this—the American flag, the flag of the state of Maryland, and the flag of the McDonald's next door, all billowing in unison in front of the fast-food restaurant against a flawless blue sky. Bliss was mine as I gazed onto my kids' favorite McDonald's while filling up my car at a gas station where the attendants know my name in small-town Maryland, transfixed by waving flags, God Bless Stability.

I did an article the summer of 1995 for the *Washington Post* called "Women at 50: Fit, Fulfilled & Blazing." I talked about Barbra Streisand and Tina Turner, Sophia Loren and Gloria Steinem, and other women of achievement who have torn through time with enviable gusto and style. Some of the subjects I interviewed, such as Zia Wesley-Hosford, author of *Fifty & Fabulous*, made me feel forty and frumpy. Her body was tiny, her skin was dewy after years of her Zia-brand wrinkle-warrior cosmetics, with a grown daughter she was free of child-rearing duties, and she was newly in love. At the age of forty-eight, Zia Hosford met her "soul mate," a man she married and with whom she had recently celebrated her fiftieth birthday strolling nude on an island paradise in the West Indies. I left the thin and sexy Wesley-Hosford, bound for the wails of four little boys in my kitchen, feeling like her grandmother. Strolling nude in the West Indies? It seemed like thousands of years ago when Chuck and I were naked in the sun on our honeymoon in St. Barts. The last woman I spoke to for this story was feminist pioneer Betty Friedan. At the age of seventy-four, Friedan sounded like I did at twenty-four:

"Somehow I have more energy than I have ever had, more sense of possibility. I keep dreaming about houses, and needing to leave one house and go to another house. There is a strong sense of being on a search and not quite knowing where it is leading."

I got many calls and notes from women in their fifties and beyond who thanked me for the article. They told me, indeed, that life had never been better. Some had just gone back to college, others had started jogging for the first time, a couple had recently gotten some great plastic surgery. They said they felt healthier than ever, hungry for new experiences, revved about taking charge of the last lap of life. And here's what I was thinking: Oh, God, Please, don't send me back on the search Betty Friedan described. I am Finally home. I don't want to leave this house and go to another house. I've been on that road to the unknown. And now, I don't crave change. I want things to stay as they are. I like this regimented pace and place. Finally, I know who I am.

Again, I am filled with thoughts of my mother, who I swore I never wanted to be. Although she was often frustrated by her domestic routine, at least there was none of the headbanging I experienced as I soared from one hot job to the next. Her days were ordered, predictable, expectations were limited, but at least they were met. Her sole job was to take care of our needs and keep us on a schedule: "You kids are my life," she would say as she put food in front of us or hugged us hard before bed. This role and home I believed to be imprisoning for my mother was actually a lot more emancipating than being faced with dozens of choices in life and love.

What I didn't know back then was that real freedom comes from knowing exactly where you are supposed to be and what you are supposed to be doing. Prison is not knowing where you are going and forever trying to get there. But who knows this until you've driven yourself mad searching? When you're always searching, you're never finding.

It is at home where the Being part of human, one's instinctive animal awareness, is awakened and fed.

To think, not that long ago I was enraptured by the worldly pursuits of Simone de Beauvoir, her lifelong fight against male oppression, her ability to love a man totally without succumbing to becoming his wife, or anyone's wife for that matter, her literary reach that extended around the globe. But then came the summer of 1995 when I read the fat biography *Simone de Beauvoir* written by Deirdre Blair and I came to know a sad woman whose writing was inflamed but whose heart-fires had been doused. From the time she was twenty-one, she loved Jean-Paul Sartre, at times carnally, always intellectually, never failing to pour herself into his work at the expense of her own, and to see him through his many illnesses. Sartre loved Simone de Beauvoir only when he needed her, discarding her at numerous stopping points for younger sexual partners and worshipful students. Because of her enduring obsession with Sartre, she could never commit to another man who loved her healthily and whom she loved back, Chicago writer Nelson Algren, author of *The Man with the Golden Arm*. Simone de Beauvoir wrote incisive, revolutionary books and filled millions of women with dreams, she filled me with dreams, and for that I am indebted. But her own saga of twisted romance and wasted time on Mr. Wrong was not any path I wanted to emulate. She was outraged at conventional female behavior, calling marriage an institution that "mutilates" women, yet she turned out to be just like a lot of the rest of us liberated females, a character out of *Women Who Love Too Much*.

Simone de Beauvoir had no children, avoiding what she called "the painful burden of pregnancy." As she told biographer Dierdre Blair: "Babies filled me with horror. The sight of a mother with a child sucking the life from her breast, or women changing soiled diapers—it all filled me with disgust. I had no desire to be drained, to be the slave to such a creature."

The man she idolized, who milked more than fifty years of her mind and soul, left control of his estate to a young, smitten woman he had officially adopted as a daughter. The shunned and bitter Nelson Algren, a man de Beauvoir called the "only truly passionate love in my life," shut off communication. And she turned into a wretched Scotch drinker, with a belly huge from cirrhosis. Stung and remorseful, the matriarch of modern feminism died in 1986 at the age of seventy-eight. Yet her trying life was fully self-determined, having done everything in her substantial powers to avoid an orthodox path. Housewifery obviously appalled her from the time she was a young woman writing sentences like this in *The Second Sex*:

"[W]hen she was a girl, the whole countryside was her homeland; the forests were hers. Now she is confined to a restricted space; Nature is reduced to the dimensions of a potted geranium; walls cut off the horizon. The home becomes the center of the world and even its only reality . . . refuge, retreat, grotto, womb, it gives shelter from outside dangers; it is this confused outer world that becomes unreal. Reality is concentrated inside the house, while outer space seems to collapse."

Refuge, retreat, grotto, womb. I consider these to be good things after too much aimless ambling in a confused outer world.

"Few tasks are more like the torture of Sisyphus than housework, with its endless repetition: the clean becomes soiled, the soiled is made clean, over and over, day after day. The housewife wears herself out marking time: she makes nothing, simply perpetuates the present. . . . Eating, sleeping, cleaning—the years no longer rise up toward heaven, they lie spread out ahead, gray and identical. . . . However respected she may be, she is subordinate, secondary, parasitic. The heavy curse that weighs upon her consists in this: the very meaning of her life is not in her hands."

Reading what sounded like a bleak forecast twenty years ago today hits me this way: the very meaning of my life is in these hands that hoist children and run a house. Repeatedly attending to endless small tasks has plunged me into the Golden Present people spend a lifetime seeking. That work is a direct path to spiritual fulfillment. Those tasks are something solid you can count on.

You cannot count on a kaleidoscope of celebrated people and exotic destinations for suspended well-being. King Hussein was on the TV news after the September 24, 1995, peace-signing ceremony that gave the Palestinians self-rule, and I told Theo that I had once talked to him at his palace. He said, "Mommy, does the king still know you?" And I said, "No, honey, he does not know me, and never did. I was a visitor." Often, on assignments, I actually felt more like a hit-and-run driver.

So what else can you count on? Four bowls of Life cereal in the morning that end up mostly on the floor. Kisses and tears and shoves and stitches and children who ask you if God has to ever cut His beard or what kind of tools He uses to make people. Mint chocolate chip ice cream dripping down tiny bare chests. Four red bicycles lined up in a row. Rapture from lying next to sleeping boys on Power Ranger flannel sheets. You can count on babies who cling to you like monkeys.

"The husband leaves in the morning, and the wife is glad to hear the door close behind him . . . she is alone . . . her hands are busy, but her mind is empty; what plans she has are for the family; she lives only for them . . ." writes de Beauvoir.

I'll take that empty calm that was once a mind riddled with strife. After years of scaling the harrowing cliffs, I am happy to be slathering grape jelly on English muffins and driving boys to Universal Gymnastics. Before I was flitting; this is living. Is there a more noble mission that trying to create whole children through surrender and love? Chuck says I hold on too tight; I tell him I can be no other way. Besides, it's the most fun I ever had—it's a matinee that never ends.

Here's one act: I am cleaning the refrigerator to a tape of James Taylor—"I've seen fire and I've seen rain. I've seen sunny days that I thought would never end"—and my boys are marching around the kitchen center island, banging pots and shouting the words to the song they hear over and over on my car stereo. And I'm taking my time to get the fridge really clean, all the glop wiped off the glass shelves, all the bruised fruit and brown lettuce and cheeses with hard edges tossed out. I frequently turn to the kids and wave my arms like a maestro and my symphony of four laugh so loudly that eight blue eyes glisten like the glass I'm buffing to a shine with a cloth diaper. And I remember the scene from *The Big Chill* where the friends from the University of Michigan, reunited fifteen years later, are dancing around the kitchen to "Please don't leave me, baby, baby," the crackle of sex in the air, high on youthful remembrances and anticipation for what's to come between old lovers flung together for a weekend.

My kitchen boogie on the river is a far different scene. I'm a grown-up now, no longer twenty-five, and experiencing that all-over-my-body crackle like the one felt at Zorine's of Chicago, a disco where a rotating silver orb sprayed fragments of light on the dance floor. The orb of light that is mine at forty-one doesn't come in darting flashes; it is a steady and nurturing beam emanating from my core, despite this dismissive judgment on being a mother and wife from de Beauvoir, a woman who never became either: ". . . bound permanently to a man, a child in her arms, she stands with her life virtually finished forever."

Bound to a man, a child in her arms—I would never have believed, when I had not one but four children in my arms, that it would signify the beginning of life, not the finale. As for sexual adventures, de Beauvoir says traditional marriage means you can kiss your erotic development good-bye. I say your sexuality gets to play out to its peak in a period of your life when you are giving birth, nursing, rocking babies, nuzzling toddlers, and sleeping with the father of your children.

When I finally relinquished my position as Wonder Woman Who Does It All and became a mother at home, actually became *my* mother, it was joy that I came to feel, not the outrage of my youth. I, too, usually have a striped kitchen towel over my shoulder, and it is a comfort, like the raggy, yellow cotton blankets are to Jack and Zane, who drag them all over the house. Strange how that kitchen towel, which once represented an object of oppression, today solidifies the fact that I am free. When a child goes down for a nap and asks me, "Mommy, will you be here when I wake up?" I say yes and I am there because I have nowhere more pressing to be, no one is expecting me, I am expecting nothing more of myself. There is nowhere else I would rather be.

Yet I haven't lost that feminist potency that Simone de Beauvoir implanted. All I have to do to get a Superwoman charge is succeed at getting four boys dressed, diaper bag packed, the crew heaped into the car, and make it through a shop at Whole Foods, where I throw organic produce into a handbasket flung over the double-stroller holding Jack and Zane. Theo and Isaac are on both sides of me, clutching my coat. Someone always stops and asks, "Are they all yours?" I take a deep breath, smile like a champion, and reply in a mighty' voice: "Yes, they are all mine." And on those occasions when they are all crying at once and I have nothing more to give, when I feel like locking myself in the closet, I call my friend Karen Chevalier and ask her how she copes as the mother of six sons, ages sixteen down to four. She reponds this way: "I thank God every day that they still want me and need me."

That priceless flicker of time when little legs and little arms grasp for dear life is changing every day, and we feel it, we know it, we mourn it, we cry. My older twin and tiniest son Jack is no longer a baby, his chubby body has stretched out, he speaks in full sentences, he drinks his juice from a cup, not a bottle. And I see the next phase of motherhood ahead, of four boys at school until 3 P.M., a phase that already leaves a lonely sting. So, In The Now, we must celebrate what is ours, and not cave in to ambitions that will still be there when the day comes that our children don't look back longingly over their shoulders as they're racing toward the school bus to join their friends.

I have changed over the years. I used to think I could do everything, that my babies would be fine squeezed into the rest of my To Do list. Today I know that children must rise to the top of the list, and that list must dwindle considerably.

When we made the choice to become mothers, we made the most elemental commitment you can make as a human being, an irrevocable promise to take care of our offspring. We were not forced to reproduce. We became mothers because we wanted to, many of us wanted this more than we have ever wanted anything else. I respect my friends who choose not to become parents because they admit to being too selfish.

I am saddened, even angry, when the act of willing pro-creation does not cause selfishness to wane.

It burns me to see how fast many high-ranking women who can well afford not to, and whose companies don't even expect them to, whip out the door back to the office within a couple of weeks—sometimes days—of delivery, armed with bat-tery-powered breast pumps to extract milk they refrigerate and save to feed newborns they've been away from all day.

I went to visit an advertising executive on a Wednesday who had given birth the Sunday before; she was planning to return to work full-time the following week. She was propped up in bed talking on a telephone that was wedged in the crook of her neck. With one hand she was holding her child to her breast, the other hand was clutching a fax just in. The phone call about a client dispute was getting her riled and she started swatting the air with the hand that had seconds earlier been securing her newborn. The baby dropped into the sea of papers that covered her bed, and as my friend ranted on, there her daughter lay, with black ink smudged on her cheek.

I have heard other new mothers one-up each other with stories of how quickly they took their first business trip, how quickly they lost the forty pounds of pregnancy weight, how quickly they were back chairing a museum benefit committee, how quickly they returned to lifting weights. As someone who has been out that door too fast before, I tell them that their old bodies and old jobs and old social selves can wait. I tell them that their infants will be in kindergarten tomorrow, and that they don't want to miss it, that they should not miss it, that it never comes back. And when they accuse me of being a hard-liner who has abandoned her feminist ideals, I assure them that there's nothing we can do more powerful as women than refuse to abandon motherhood.

I know that I have more choices than many other mothers of young children. Yet I also believe that most women have more choices then they think they have, starting with the choice of when to conceive a child.

I think of my friend Grace, an exquisite portrait artist, who recently got an inquiry from the governor's office to paint the first lady of the state. Grace did not even pursue this lead, or follow up on the stream of offers she constantly gets from prestigious Washington galleries to show her work. She is frequently asked to teach college courses, but these requests are also turned down. At this stage of her life, she does not want a bigger career. She wants to be with her children, ages six and four. She keeps up a streamlined profession while the kids are in school by working eight hours a week in her studio doing portraits for local clients.

For this decision, her family is "practically poor," living on her artist's salary and income from her husband, Paul, a horticulturist. They rent a small house, their living room is furnished with an antique couch that Paul found abandoned in an alley, they drive an old Jeep handed down by an uncle, and Grace loves her life:

"I never sit down and say, 'Oh, we've got to get out there and make more money.' We made so little money last year, but we made it honestly and we feel so rich. I am here all the time for these kids and they are turning out well. They are not plunked in front of a TV by a baby-sitter. They are baking and they are taking hikes and they are playing with me. You know, there's nothing wrong with the way we were raised in the fifties and sixties."

Grace laughs when she recalls the day a twenty-year-old girlfriend came for lunch, bringing a poster of Gloria Steinem, whom she had just heard speak at her college. The young woman was going on and on about the glory of female power and liberation, and while Grace listened she was washing dishes, cleaning the counters, wiping up the floor, and starting to shuck corn for that night's dinner.

"My friend was looking at me shocked," says Grace. "She asked me, 'Why are you cooking dinner already? We just finished lunch.' And I told her, 'Honey, this is what you have to look forward to someday.' And I think it just blew her away, because in her mind kitchen duty is not something that a strong and liberated woman would do. We didn't think that either."

Disillusioned by old heroes who instructed me to avoid kitchen duty at all costs, my primary inspiration today comes from other mothers like Grace with benched hot careers, friends like Charlene Quinn, mother of six-year-old Danny and one-year-old Katherine. I spent a spring afternoon on a bank by the Chesapeake Bay with Charlene eating three-inch strawberries from her garden, drinking orange Hi-C, and watching our boys hurl driftwood onto the rocks at water's edge. She used to be a White House fellow specializing in health care, assigned to prepare a study of catastrophic illness during the Reagan administration, and she has been doing course work toward a Ph.D. at Johns Hopkins University since 1981, which she is inches away from completing.

The sun of early May beating down on us, Charlene told me that she had just gotten a call from a former colleague asking if she wanted to become a freelance health-care adviser to Newt Gingrich. Charlene turned it down: "I'm too busy," she explained. With baby Katherine grabbing at her juice-box straw, Charlene giggled over what she was so busy doing—sewing costumes for Danny's class play. She said that she loved to sew and hadn't done it for years, because she had been too engrossed in her job.

I thought about the word *busy*, defined as "engaged in action" or "occupied." In my single, turbocharged life I kept busy because I was running away from myself. But being busy with children means something entirely different: Engaged in action, occupied by their limbs and needs, I am joyful to deaccelerate and be Where I Am and Who I Am.

That night, as I cracked eggs and crumbled Ritz crackers into the meat loaf mixture, I thought about all the other good stuff we get to be busy with in this blink of life at home with young children. Like watch the Flintstones at 5:43 A.M. Eat pastel dot candy off paper. Dig up worms. Live close to the bone with no makeup on and knots in your hair and calamine caked on your legs to stem the itch from bites you get on hunts through the woods for dinosaur bones. Twirl around the living room with four worshipful little guys to Wee Sing's version of "Rock My Soul in the Bosom of Abraham."

Stand in silence at the foot of your stairs after the children are in bed, a Batman umbrella at your feet, and knowing, finally, It's All Here, Right Here, Right Now, yours, moment after moment of Divine Radiance: "You Are All Form, You Are the Breath, You Are the River, You Are the Void, Be Here Now." Ram Dass, I'm there.

I'm there with Theo as he rides a fat Shetland named Ziggy at a nearby farm in Davidsonville, Maryland. The air smells like dirt and manure and winter, and my little boy is learning how to hold the reins and trot and turn against the backdrop of a russet red barn and an aged silver silo. He is good on that pony, and he knows it, because he keeps looking at me to make sure I'm looking at him. I am so grateful to be shivering on a cold wooden bench a few yards away so he can see my eyes gleam with love and pride. I am thinking about riding Chico as a young girl at the Double U Ranch in Tucson, Arizona, where tobacco-spitting cowboys led us on trails through cactus in the desert, and how I couldn't wait to get back so my mother and father, who would be waiting at the corral, could see me strong and sure in the saddle.

That went a long way.

BIBLIOGRAPHY

The Holy Bible: New International Version

Cliffe, Albert E. *Let Go and Let God*. New Jersey: Prentice-Hall, 1951

Colson, Charles. *Born Again*. Grand Rapids, MI: Chosen Books, 1977

Cromartie, Michael, ed. *The Nine Lives of Population Control*. Grand Rapids, MI: Eerdmans, 1995

Dass, Baba Ram. *Be Here Now*. New York: Crown, 1971

De Beauvoir, Simone. *The Second Sex*. New York: Vintage Books, 1990

Eisenberg, Arlene. *What to Expect When You're Expecting*. New York: Workman, 1991

Fallaci, Oriana. *Interview with History*. Boston: Houghton Mifflin, 1977

Faludi, Susan. *Backlash: The Undeclared War Against Women*. Landover Hills, MD: Anchor Publishing, 1992

Friedan, Betty. *The Feminine Mystique*. New York: Dell Publishing, 1984

Graham, Billy. *Peace with God*. Dallas: Word Publishing, 1984

Greer, Germaine. *The Female Eunuch*. New York: McGraw-Hill, 1971

Hansel, Tim. *You Gotta Keep Dancin'*. Elgin, IL: Chariot Family, 1986

Harayda, Janice. *The Joy of Being Single*. New York: Doubleday, 1986

Herrigel, Eugen. *Zen in the Art of Archery*. New York: Vintage Books, 1989

Jong, Erica. *Fear of Flying*. New York: Signet, 1974

Keyes, Ken Jr. *Handbook to Higher Consciousness*. Love Line Books, 1975

Kierkegaard, Søren. *The Sickness Unto Death*. New York: Penguin Books, 1989

Krishnamurti, J. *Freedom from the Known*. Harper San Francisco, 1975

Leach, Penelope. *Your Baby & Child*. New York: Knopf, 1989

Lewis, C.S. *Mere Christianity*. New York: Collier, 1952

Miller, Arthur. *Death of a Salesman*. New York: Penguin Books, 1972

Moore, Thomas. *Soul Mates: Honoring the Mysteries of Love & Relationships.* New York: HarperCollins, 1994

Peale, Ruth. *The Adventure of Being a Wife.* New Jersey: Prentice-Hall, 1971

Peck, M. Scott. *The Road Less Traveled.* New York: Touchstone Books, 1988

Prather, Hugh and Gayle. *I Will Never Leave You: How Couples Can Achieve the Power of Lasting Love.* New York: Bantam, 1995

Salzberg, Sharon. *Loving Kindness: The Revolutionary Art of Happiness.* Boston: Shambhala, 1995

Sartre, Jean-Paul. *Nausea.* New York: New Directions, 1959

Schacter-Shalomi, Zalman, with Donald Gropman. *The First Step: A Guide for the New Jewish Spirit.* New York: Bantam, 1983

Spock, Benjamin. *Baby and Child Care.* New York: Dutton, 1946

Suzuki, Shunryu. *Zen Mind, Beginner's Mind.* New York: Weatherhill, 1970

Thevenin, Tine. *The Family Bed.* Self-published, 1976

Thoreau, Henry David. *Walden, or Life in the Woods.* New York: Penguin Books, 1983

Wiesel, Elie. *Night.* New York: Bantam, 1982

Yogananda, Paramahansa. *Metaphysical Meditations.* Self-Realization Fellowship, 1964